In Memory of

Martine Franck

(1938–2012)

Photographer and Wife
of Henri Cartier-Bresson

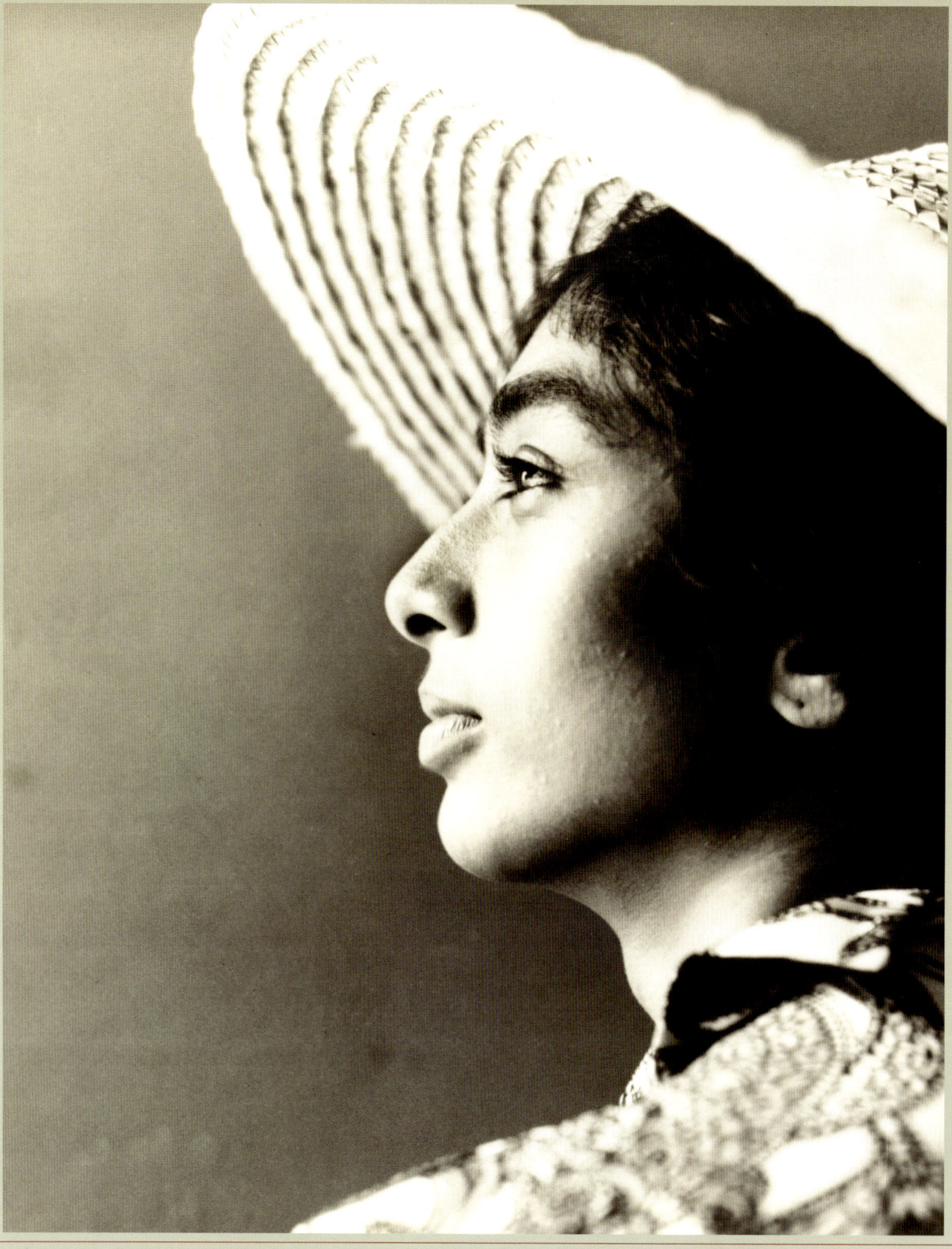

MASTERING THE LENS

BEFORE AND AFTER CARTIER-BRESSON IN PONDICHERRY

INTRODUCTIONS BY

H.E. Mr François Richier
THE FRENCH AMBASSADOR TO INDIA

E. Alkazi
CHAIRMAN, ALKAZI FOUNDATION FOR THE ARTS

CURATED BY

Rahaab Allana

WITH TEXT CONTRIBUTIONS BY

Shilpi Goswami
Deepak Bharathan
Prof. Kittu Reddy and
Jennifer Chowdhry

MAPIN PUBLISHING IN ASSOCIATION WITH THE ALKAZI COLLECTION OF PHOTOGRAPHY
SUPPORTED BY THE EMBASSY OF FRANCE, INDIA, AND ALLIANCE FRANÇAISE DE DELHI

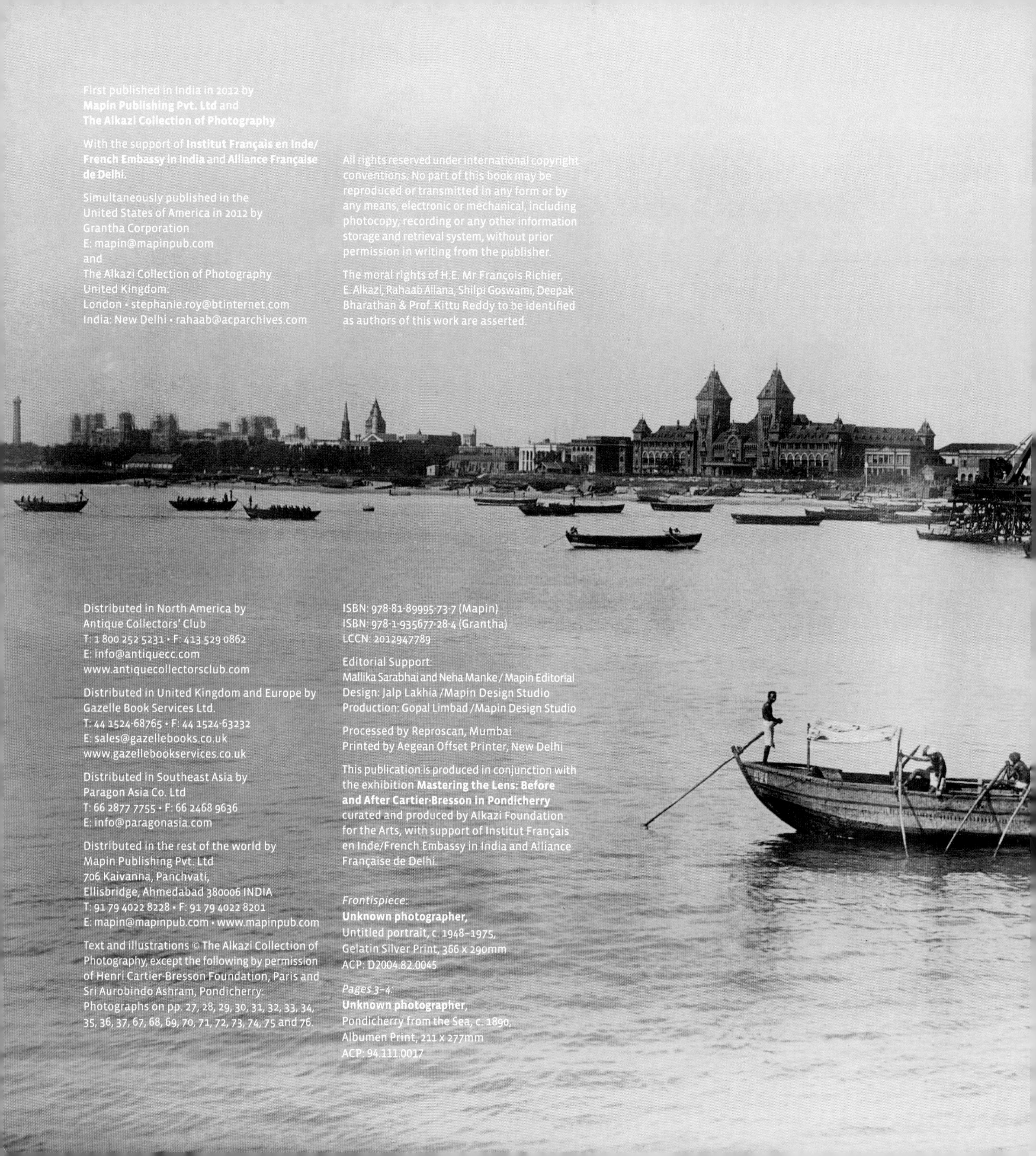

First published in India in 2012 by
Mapin Publishing Pvt. Ltd and
The Alkazi Collection of Photography

With the support of **Institut Français en Inde/ French Embassy in India** and **Alliance Française de Delhi.**

Simultaneously published in the
United States of America in 2012 by
Grantha Corporation
E: mapin@mapinpub.com
and
The Alkazi Collection of Photography
United Kingdom:
London • stephanie.roy@btinternet.com
India: New Delhi • rahaab@acparchives.com

Distributed in North America by
Antique Collectors' Club
T: 1 800 252 5231 • F: 413 529 0862
E: info@antiquecc.com
www.antiquecollectorsclub.com

Distributed in United Kingdom and Europe by
Gazelle Book Services Ltd.
T: 44 1524-68765 • F: 44 1524-63232
E: sales@gazellebooks.co.uk
www.gazellebookservices.co.uk

Distributed in Southeast Asia by
Paragon Asia Co. Ltd
T: 66 2877 7755 • F: 66 2468 9636
E: info@paragonasia.com

Distributed in the rest of the world by
Mapin Publishing Pvt. Ltd
706 Kaivanna, Panchvati,
Ellisbridge, Ahmedabad 380006 INDIA
T: 91 79 4022 8228 • F: 91 79 4022 8201
E: mapin@mapinpub.com • www.mapinpub.com

ISBN: 978-81-89995-73-7 (Mapin)
ISBN: 978-1-935677-28-4 (Grantha)
LCCN: 2012947789

Editorial Support:
Mallika Sarabhai and Neha Manke / Mapin Editorial
Design: Jalp Lakhia /Mapin Design Studio
Production: Gopal Limbad /Mapin Design Studio

Processed by Reproscan, Mumbai
Printed by Aegean Offset Printer, New Delhi

This publication is produced in conjunction with the exhibition **Mastering the Lens: Before and After Cartier-Bresson in Pondicherry** curated and produced by Alkazi Foundation for the Arts, with support of Institut Français en Inde/French Embassy in India and Alliance Française de Delhi.

Frontispiece:
Unknown photographer,
Untitled portrait, c. 1948–1975,
Gelatin Silver Print, 366 x 290mm
ACP: D2004.82.0045

Pages 3–4:
Unknown photographer,
Pondicherry from the Sea, c. 1890,
Albumen Print, 211 x 277mm
ACP: 94.111.0017

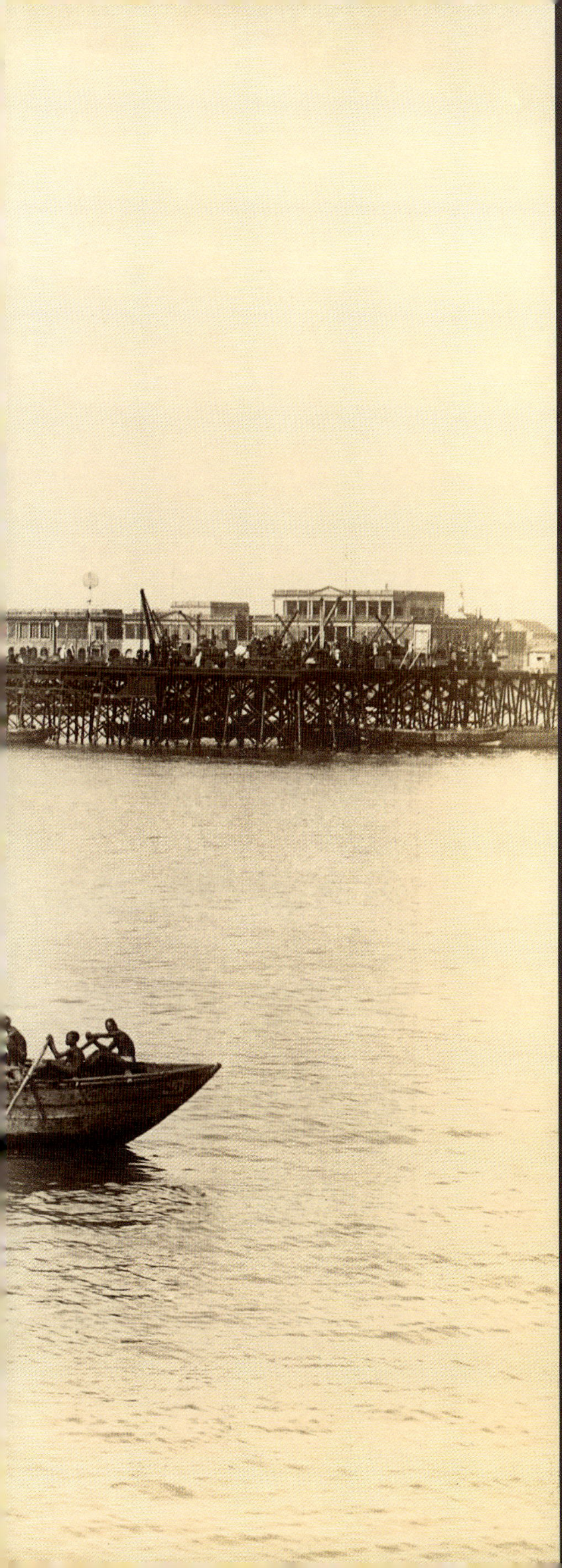

RENEWING TIES

LINKING INDIA AND FRANCE THROUGH THE ART OF PHOTOGRAPHY

H.E. Mr François Richier
THE FRENCH AMBASSADOR TO INDIA

India and France have a shared history of mutual fascination and reciprocal influences through commercial and cultural exchanges dating back to the 17th century. It started with the first meeting between French explorers and Indian maharajahs; and was to continue in the 20th century with the friendship forged between André Malraux, the French Minister of Culture, and Jawaharlal Nehru.

The exchange of ideas is most evident in Pondicherry, where the first French merchants had set foot, producing a unique cultural melting pot, which includes original architecture, a deep-rooted attachment to French language and many other legacies within the framework of arts. More than any other place, Pondicherry has always been a gateway to new perspectives of self-development, artistic fulfilment and intellectual enrichment, particularly for French people who are attracted to Indian culture, philosophy and spirituality.

An epitome of this tradition was the meeting of famous French photographer Henri Cartier-Bresson and one of India's most important philosophers of the 20th century, Sri Aurobindo together with his companion, Mirra Alfassa—"the Mother". Cartier-Bresson had just founded Magnum Photos agency, with other great French photographers such as Robert Capa and David Seymour, and soon achieved international recognition. In the aftermath of the World War II, he had become the leader of a photography movement that replaced the old tradition of over-sophisticated and over-posed images—by shooting vivid glimpses of real life, be they historical events or day-to-day occupations, transcending the bounderies between art and journalism.

His quest for new challenges and self-improvement led him to India several times, where he even met Mahatma Gandhi in 1947. In 1950, thanks to the Mother's intervention, he was able to visit Aurobindo Ashram, where he took some of the photographs presented in this publication, a few months before Sri Aurobindo's death.

For too long, these pictures had remained unheralded. But thanks to the work of the Alkazi Foundation, they are now available to an enlarging audience. Over the last 30 years, Mr E. Alkazi has privately gathered pictures from the 19th and 20th centuries, revealing lesser-known aspects of Indian socio-economic, political or cultural history, not only to scholars but also, through various exhibitions to a larger public. France is honoured and pleased to have now brought to light, through Cartier-Bresson's eye and earlier works from the archive, the ambivalent poetic spell of Pondicherry's old times.

At a time when the world is undergoing a major transformation, where globalisation through cultural exchanges is reaching an unprecedented level, these pictures of Cartier-Bresson are a beautiful meditation on what France and India, two different and ancient cultures, can learn from each other—primarily the universality of art and spirituality. That was certainly what Emperor Ashoka thought when he wrote, more than 2000 years ago: "I am proud of my humanity every time I appreciate poets and artists from other countries than mine".

THE ENDURING IMAGE

E. Alkazi
CHAIRMAN, ALKAZI FOUNDATION FOR THE ARTS

The history of photography in India is fundamentally linked to the French invention of the medium in the 19th century, and the pioneering discovery of Sir Nicéphore Niépce (1765-1833) who simply produced a 'view' through his window in 1826 by use of a *camera obscura*. Less than two decades hence, the medium gradually establishes itself in India exposing the vast expanse of her territories and the diversity of its people as part of a continuing visual tradition. At an art historical level, the production of small format, easily portable photographs are also reminiscent of the Mughal miniature paintings that revealed the lyrical intensity of a patron's enduring image on paper. Both occurrences, painting and then photography, though separated by the continuum of time, manner and perhaps intent, mark a cultural collision that has evolved into the present state of photography as a cultural tool and an incisive form of expression.

Some of the early French photographers in India include Alex de la Grange (born 1825), and Oscar Malitte (1829-1905) who captured not only architectural splendours but the humanity that steered India from a colony to an independent nation. It is with homage to them and their contemporaries that an archive of images from the 19th century becomes part of our collective legacy and heritage. At a more conceptual level, photography developed two adjacent lives: the first as a testament to reality, and the other as an abiding practice of the arts. Both lives were equally viable and deeply in tune with the modern demands of photography: to challenge reality and to explore the abstractions of human imagination.

Romanticism as an aesthetic position was introduced and then transgressed by some of the leading French photographers of their time: Henri le Sec and Jean Paul Gaude, the portraiture of Nadar and the urban modernism of Eugene Atget. This later evolves into the social documentary photograph, a leading practitioner of which is Henri Cartier Bresson (1908-2004). Though his time in India has been well documented, the events that transpired in Pondicherry, namely at the Sri Aurobindo Ashram in the 1950s remain an obscure part of photo-histories. Reproduced in this catalogue for the first time the images here were collaborative, as Bresson envisioned them with the guidance of the Mother, and the consent of Sri Aurobindo himself.

The 1960s mark the coming of age of modern photography in India with an unprecedented number of practitioners, often anonymous, who were near contemporaries of Bresson. Once again, the Aurobindo Ashram comes to the fore highlighting a forgotten period of experimentation and practice. Varied initiatives of photography begin to emerge, taking from pictorial traditions in fine art and re-examining them with the lens. The unique blend of French and Indian sensibilities allows for a more expanded understanding of the influence of photography at a practical and discursive level.

The world of photography thus enters an enlarged arena of artistic influences, forged as part of its global initiative: its ability, today, to draw in people and spaces from different cultures into a common purview and engender a creative response. This exhibition is then an exploration of lesser-known, but extremely illuminating works from the visual archives of the Alkazi Collection, with which we envisage new frontiers of research, and renewed ways of linking photographers and artists to their times, as well as to the present. We are therefore grateful to the Embassy of France, India, as well as the Alliance Française de Delhi for collaborating with us at an institutional level and consolidating alliances for the future of our two nations.

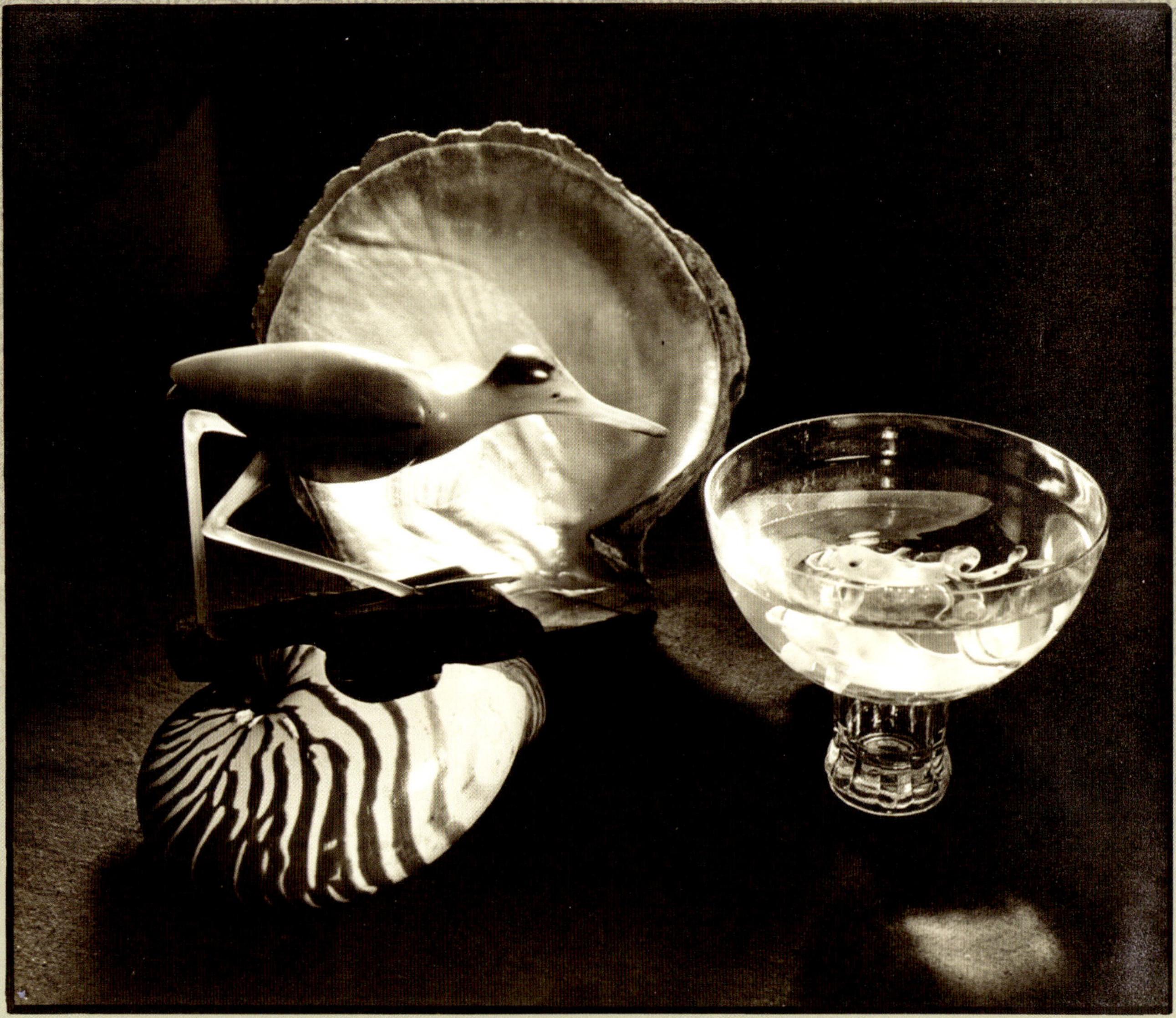

Venkatesh Shirodkar
Sri Aurobindo Ashram, Pondicherry, c. 1948–1975,
Illusion, Gelatin Silver Print, 245 x 291 mm,
Rolleiflex Automat—Tessar F.3,5;1/2 Sec. at F.8. Dev. in D.K. 20;
Enlarged on Bromesko
ACP: D2004.82.0008

I really believe there are things nobody would see
if I didn't photograph them.

Diane Arbus

SILENT AS AN APPARITION

A Hidden Legacy of Photography

Rahaab Allana

Bresson may have uttered the same words with reference to his rare, self-commissioned album featuring 119 images emerging from Aurobindo Ashram in Pondicherry. Instead, his careful observations about the Ashram as well as the city, generously provided by the Henri Cartier-Bresson Foundation in Paris brings forth a hidden reserve of photo-history, untouched by the scholarly world or viewed by practitioners. Bresson meticulously pens his thoughts, occasionally jotting down segments of his conversations with the French-born leader of Auroville, commonly known as 'The Mother', who meanders in and out of his frames, 'silent as an apparition'. Her 'strong, kind and fascinating eyes' prompt a personal, if not biographical, perspective on photography history.

At approximately the same time in India, photographers like Margaret Bourke White were traveling with (the late) Sunil Janah, while others like Shambu Saha were developing a form of Industrial photography. However, upon further investigation, we have discovered that Pondicherry too underwent a visual 'worlding' that marks a crucial moment in the development of photography here. The Ashram harboured young talent by providing state of the art equipment, and in the form of an annual Salon Festival for almost 25 years (c.1955-80). The kinds of photos that were submitted and selected explored a dialogue on artistic intent and reception, with evidence of a continuing aesthetic of 'pictorial' photography—a predominant form tied to the formal aspects of fine art.

This was a curatorial route into the past, through 'media' and the conceptual linking of mannerisms and tropes. The geographical region itself had been visited by visual artists from the 17th century, who documented it's serene vistas—brought to life as an amalgamation of Christian and local elements in architecture and urban sprawl. The use of antiquarian maps from the 18th and 19th century reveals an intricately Europeanised town, though structurally segregated, featuring a shared use of motifs and style. The arrival of commercial photographers Bourne and Shepherd, or indeed mysterious French photographer, Charles Moyne uncovers an expansive city of citadels and churches.

The unearthing of archival material is balanced by a few surviving photographers from the 1960s, some of whom have been recently interviewed. As with vintage photographs, modern landscape photographers in the Aurobindo Ashram carry on the legacy of image-making into the 20th century. The temporal jump from the 19th to the 20th century is exemplified through extraordinary images of Indian practitioners such as Tara Jauhar and Sri Venkatesh at Aurobindo Ashram. The photographers though distinct in their technique, express how personal narratives were encouraged as part of project-based shoots. However the presentation of an album by Bresson in conjunction with this work can be considered a notional extension, showcasing his more 'amateur' experiments at a time when photographers were playfully tempering light and contrast; a form of 'artistic darkness' for instance that Bresson was asked to consider upon instruction from the Mother while shooting Sri Aurobindo during *darshan*.

This exhibition addresses how photographers changed the course of photography with stylistic 'departures' during the 1950s and 60s, whilst using images from the 19th century to examine a sense of lineage. The archive is positioned to support the coming of modernity, by way of an iconographic association. The forces at play at a compositional level as well as those of patronage and practice manage to fulfill the claims made on photography by amateur photographers trying relentlessly to infuse a subjective manner in their practices. Though such ventures stand in contrast to more mainstream journalistic forays, which Bresson is acclaimed for, we witness an intended 'shift' in temperament and focus from the 19th century: an abounding personal commentary, largely devoid of commercial intent—which inadvertently influences the known legacies of photography in India.

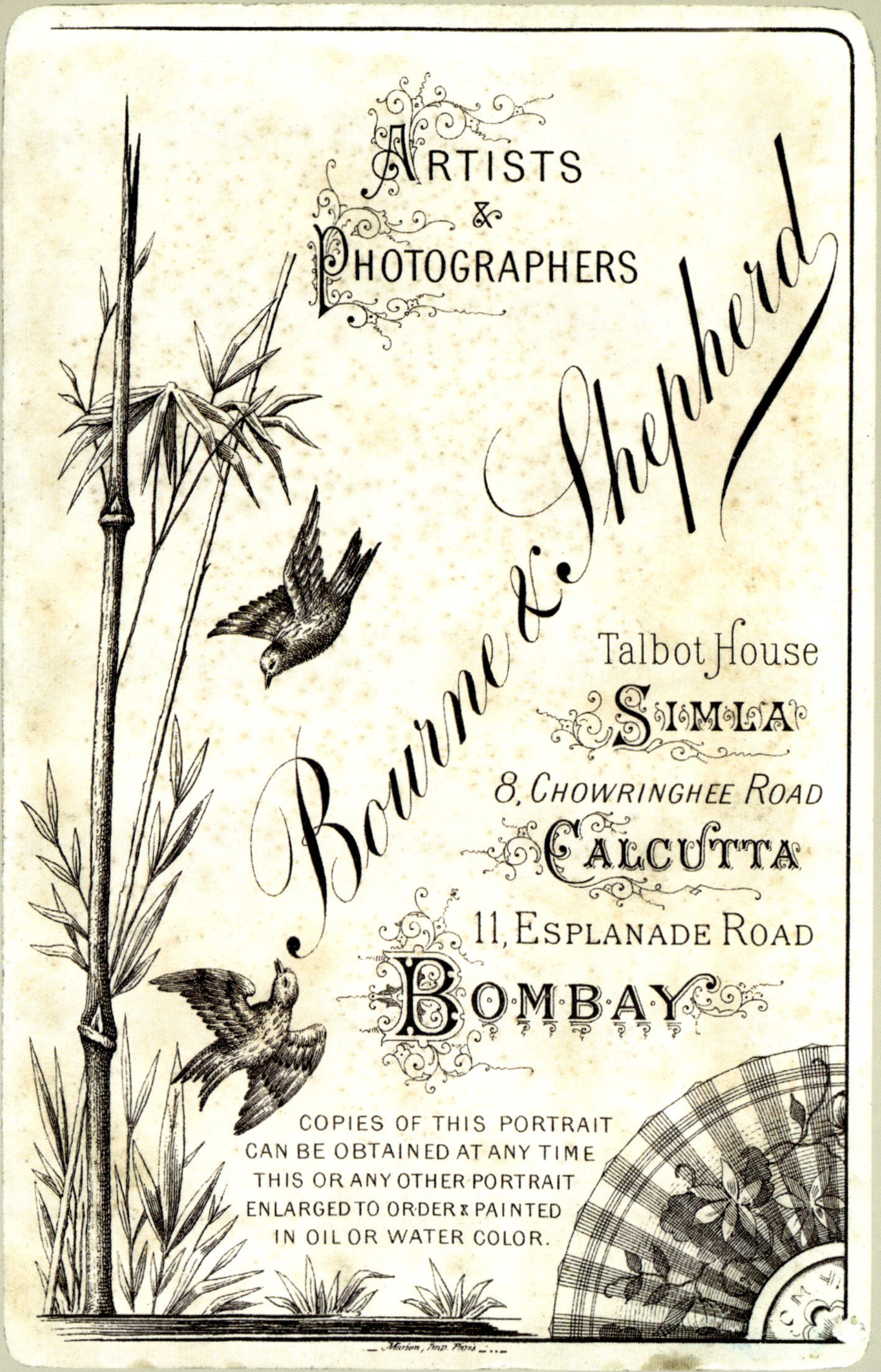

Bourne & Shepherd
11, Esplanade Road, Bombay, c. 1880–1890
Verso of Cabinet Card, 165 x 110 mm,
ACP: 94.75.0004

MASTERING THE LENS

Before and After Cartier-Bresson in Pondicherry

Shilpi Goswami and Deepak Bharathan

"The power—and authority—of the visual in modern Indian public sphere emerges from the fact that it inhabits such an 'interocular' or 'intervisual' field, overlapping, intersecting, and interlocking with other images and in conjuncture with different media, triggering associations, catalyzing memories, rendering the unfamiliar recognizable, and frequently reconfiguring the recognizable, so that, as earlier images.... [they] are forever waiting to erupt in the present as they continually migrate, moving in and out of new times and changing political contexts."

Sumathi Ramaswamy[1]

The intellectual charge of the statement above lies in its recognition of the complexities involved in the development of media strategies, especially at a nascent stage of intercultural relations occurring in the colonial period. Photography as a form of reportage, as well as individual perception undergoes a 'worlding' in India, based on its progressions, influences and manifestations across all spheres of socio-political activity.

Photography emerged in India shortly after the public announcement of the Calotype in London and Daguerreotype's invention in 1839 in Paris. From 1840 onwards, the governments of imperial nations realised its potential for recording the antiquities of the 'Orient'. Other European photographers in India at the time such as Samuel Bourne (1834–1912) or the French aristocrat-photographer Baron Alexis Aimé de La Grange (1825–1917) captured the essence of photography's nascent use: a form of reportage, documentation and inventory keeping. The story of early photography in India is hence deeply aligned to the influence of European culture eastwards, primarily as a technology that was introduced in Calcutta, one of the principal states of the British Presidency, as early as 1840.[2] The rise of photography in India, practiced both inside and outside the studio, offers not only a fascinating social history of its patronage, usage and circulation, but also its transition to an art form and practice, underscoring the need for a deeper investigation of the challenges it faced and developments it wrought on visual culture, then as well as now.[3]

Photography was taken up with alacrity by amateurs, aspirant professionals, commercial practitioners as well as by the apparatus of the colonial state.[4] The 1860s witnessed many pioneers arriving in the subcontinent and establishing long-standing firms during this time, and soon Bombay (Mumbai), Calcutta (Kolkata) and Madras (Chennai) developed their own unique photographic societies. However, the lineage provided by the medium does not only present evidence of mainstream studios in larger metropolitan cities, but also of vernacular traditions and experiments that help to deconstruct its effect on the subcontinent as a whole. A reference to ateliers of artists, who later interacted with photography in Rajasthan, substantiates this notion, elucidated in another publication on *Painted Photographs*[5] from the Alkazi Collection.

The function of a popular or emancipated tradition in India therefore arises out of the conversation between tradition and modernity, the past and the continuing present. Hence the notion of a 'cannon' in photography history here is fraught with ambivalences, bearing in mind the growing exposure of new (often private) archives or indeed the juxtaposition of visual archives with oral or textual works. It is also important then to reconsider the terms 'popular', 'traditional' and 'mainstream' as personal albums of photography also highlight the tastes and aesthetic predications of a generation or indeed, an era.[6]

The following article hence volunteers thus-far unpublished material, for the most part, in this case from Pondicherry, housed in The Alkazi Collection of Photography. It is an attempt to unearth the 'lesser-known' visual history of the city, deeply inspired by the coming of the French. The use of archival material such as vintage maps provide a holistic view of the city and the early rise of the French influence here, followed by references to the 19th century images that visualise vast landscapes through aerial and linear images of the city. However, at the crux of the article, beyond the domains of the 'vintage' archive, lies a modern history of the medium seen through the compelling images of Cartier-Bresson in the Sri Aurobindo Ashram. Surprisingly, we found that the Sri Aurobindo Ashram also supported photography in the 1950s and 60s, and some of the practitioners are still living. Consequently, if the 1950s are seen as a point of refraction in the development of photography in India, the archive of images presented here will enliven Sumathi Ramaswamy's assertion about how cultural histories and art practices inevitably collide in order to redraft the past.

THE FRENCH IN PONDICHERRY

Pondicherry, a port city on the Coromandel Coast[7] has been home to the various cultures and communities, drawn to it as a trading zone. The Portuguese were some of the first foreign settlers here, who arrived in 1521 to trade in cotton textiles. Like any other commercial centre, there gradually developed a unique infrastructure, seen in the architecture and customs. The Dutch, the Danes and the French followed suit in the 17th century transforming the city into a unique blend of European and local cultural norms. The maps and photographs identified in this section therefore help to piece together the urban spread of the city as a whole [Fig.1].

The French were primarily drawn to Pondicherry for the manufacture of fine cloth, as both cotton and indigo grew abundantly in the countryside. A weaver's village existed north of White Town in the late 1690s. Francois Martin, who founded Pondicherry, invited weavers and painters to the city in 1674 and they built 40 houses on a plot of land granted to them. The weavers sector of Pondicherry quickly developed into one of the picturesque locations within the town, with craftsmen working under a broad stretch of trees planted meaningfully along the avenues.[8] According to S.J. Stephen, professor of maritime history and an author, the Dutch plan of 1694 shows that '*many streets of the weavers, washers, painters, silver-smiths, coppersmiths, carpenters, hookers, trumpeters, shepherds, oil mongers, rope makers and barbers came into existence in the inner structure of the town. The grid was so designed as to keep each section of the inhabitants in their separate places*'[9] [Fig. 2].

In 1761, Pondicherry fell to the British who completely destroyed the city and its many architectural works including Dupleix's[10] Government House. The Anglo-French conflicts continued till 1816 when Pondicherry was finally ceded to the French.[11]

Following its destruction by the English, Pondicherry was reconstructed within the existing limits of the town and most of the private houses were built on their old sites. However there were many significant changes in the layout and structure that can be seen in vintage photographs from the region. The town was divided into two parts by a canal, which separated the European quarter from the Indian residents who had devised their own manner of living[12] [Fig.3 & 4]. The Indian quarter was characterized by a Tamil style of architecture with *thalvaram* (street verandah with a platform and lean-to-roof over wooden posts) and a *thinnai* (semi-public verandah space with masonry benches for visitors).[13]

The French town on the other hand was characterized by a European classical style comparable with Parisian villas, high compound walls, elaborate gates, garden courts, arched patios, colonnaded galleries, voluminous rooms, high arched openings, and wooden balconies with flat terraced roofs, developed along the coastline around the Government Square. Stately buildings

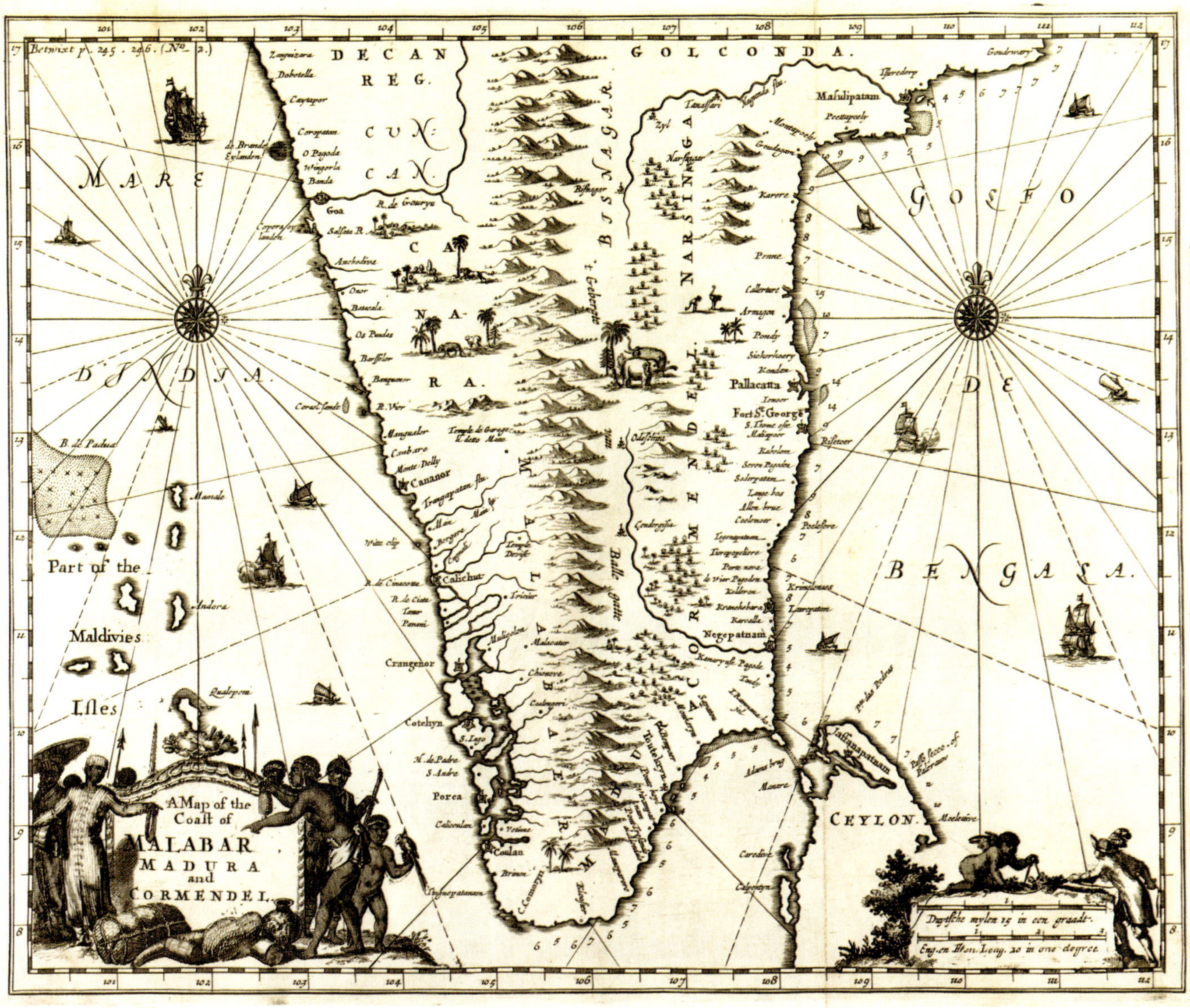

Fig. 1
A Map of the Coast of Malabar, Madura and Cormendel, c. 1700, Ink on Paper, 316 x 399 mm
ACP: 2012.01.M1

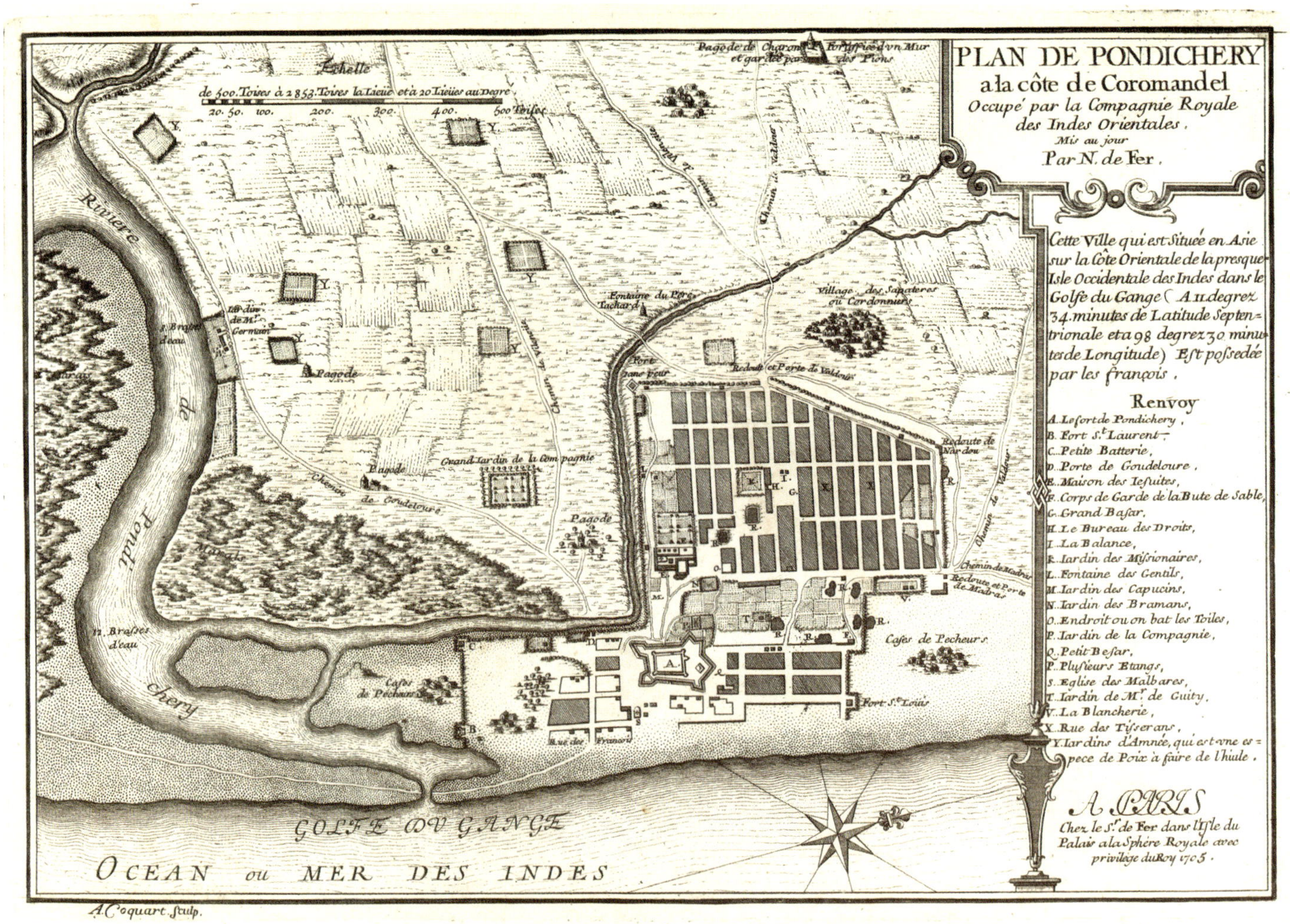

Fig. 2

Nicolas De Fer

Plan de Pondichery a la côte de Coromandel Occupé par la Compagnie Royale de Indes Orientales (Map of Pondicherry on the Coromandel Coast occupied by the Royal East India Company), 1705

Ink on Paper, 239 x 353 mm

ACP: 2012.01.M2

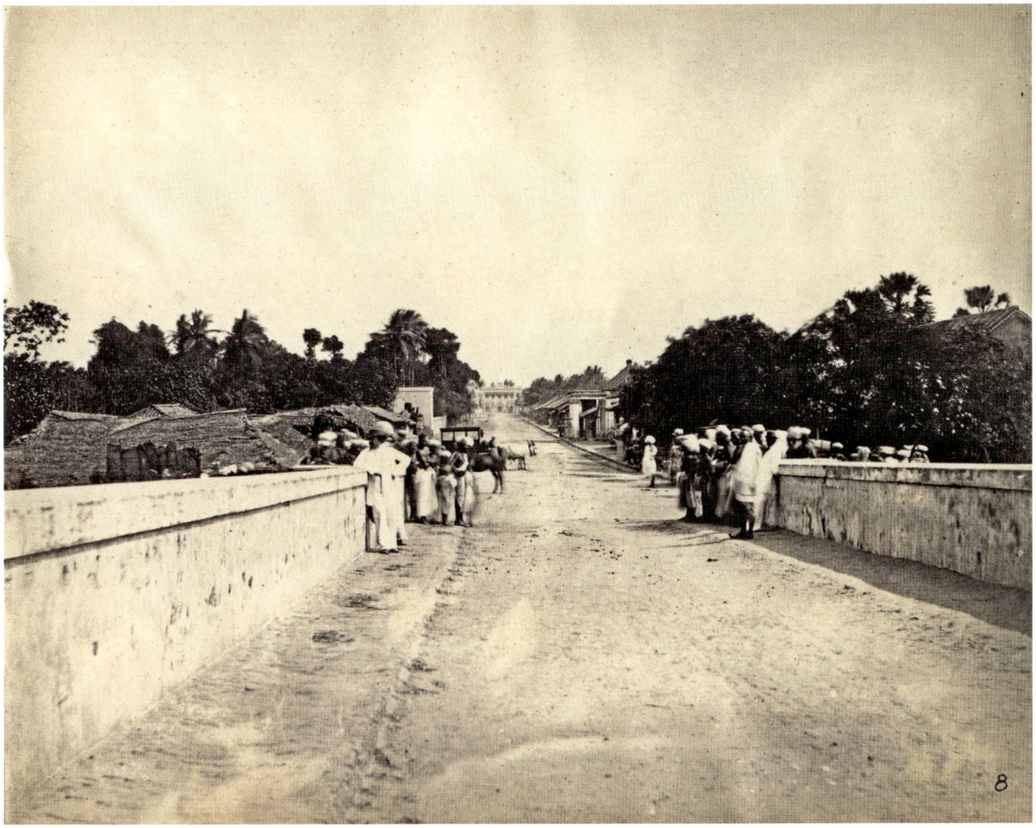

Fig. 3
Unknown Photographer
Principal Street, Karical
(currently Karaikal), c. 1860
Albumen Print, Photographer's Ref. 8,
193 x 243 mm
ACP: 97.16.0079(0003)

Karaikal is a small coastal enclave within the Union Territory, about 130 km south of the city. It was formerly part of French India.

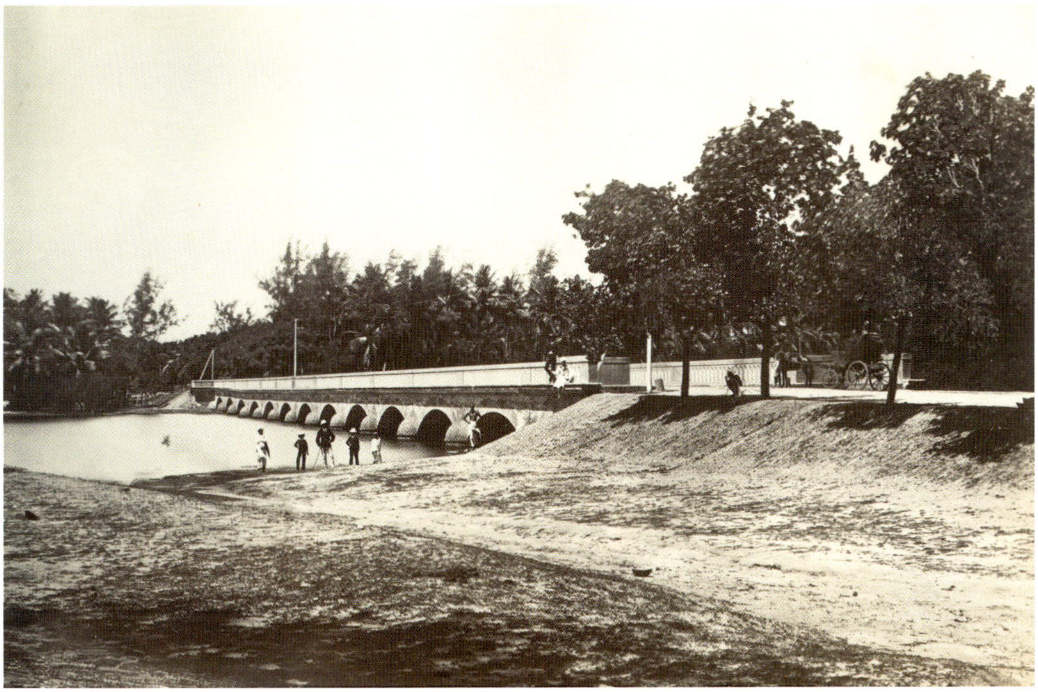

Fig. 4
Unknown Photographer
Areuncoupom Bridge-Pondichery
(Ariyankuppam Bridge), c. 1880
Albumen Print, 141 x 218 mm
ACP: 97.48.0001(0049)

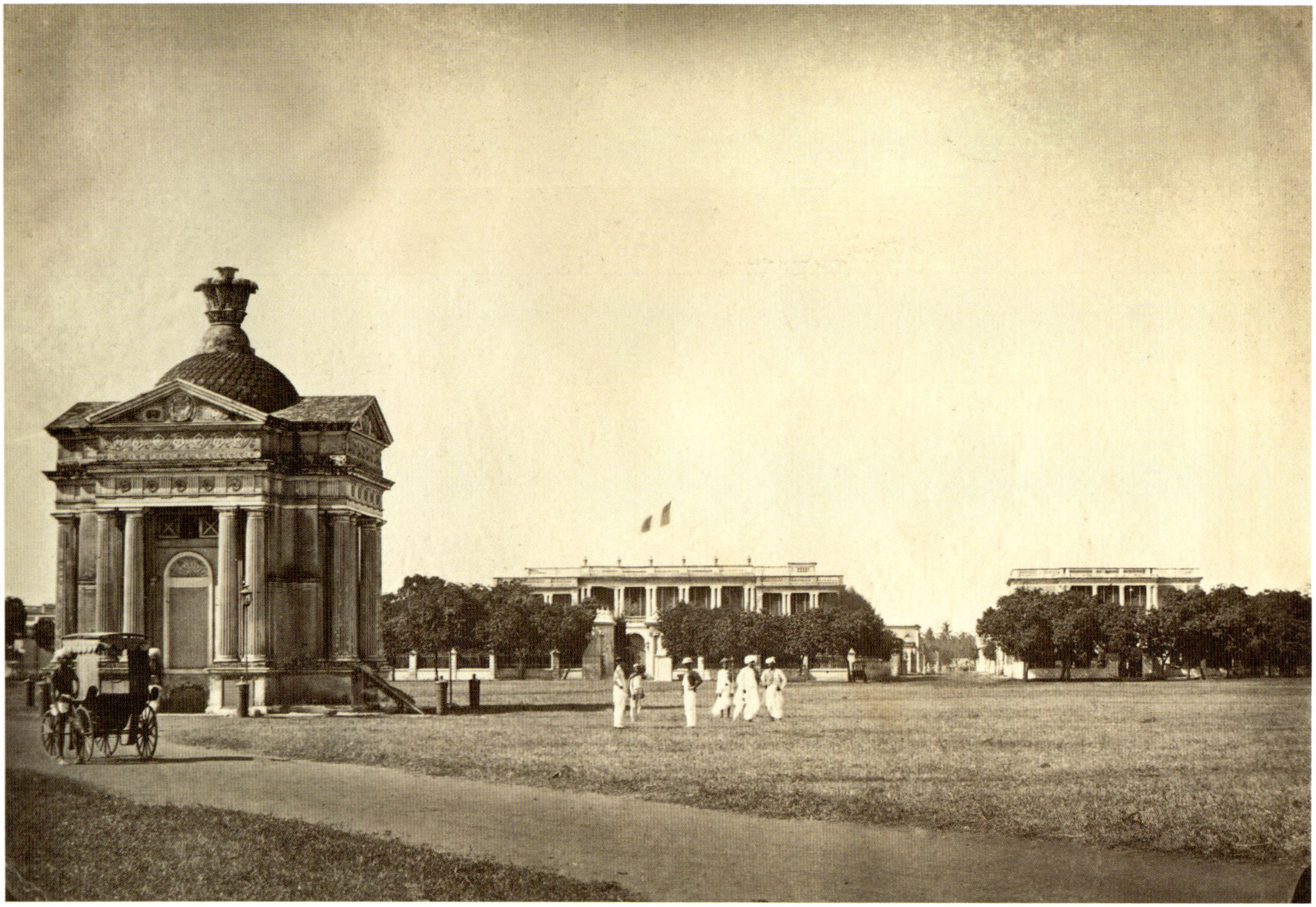

such as the Customs House, Tribunal Court and other impressive structures surrounded the Square itself.[14] The Government House [Fig. 5] was reconstructed, designed by Monsieur Dumont in the Tuscan-Doric style with Rococo style interiors.[15] Bourçet, the engineer responsible for the reconstruction, designed the house in a much less grand scale, transforming the Baroque-Classism into a neo-Classicism style.[16]

In the centre of the European quarter was the parade ground of the old citadel [Fig. 6]. It was planted with trees, with boulevards and canals, and on its four sides were new government buildings - the Governor's Palace and the Administrative office on the north, warehouses on the south, and military barracks on the east and west. The streets were all straight, stretching from east to west and from north to south cutting each other at right angles.[17] The entire town was hence laid out in planned grids. Buildings like Hôtel du Gouvernement, the Palais de Justice, Messageries Maritimes were built in 1862 [Fig. 7], and the Aayi Mandapam was constructed in 1863 [Fig. 8]. A lighthouse was installed on the seashore and a pier was built between 1835 and 1866 [Fig. 9]. The statue of Dupleix was installed in 1870 [Fig. 10] and a railway line was laid from Pondicherry to Villupuram in 1879.[18]

Though the early development of photography in the region is unclear, some surviving images cited in the text provide a sense of the agendas and intentionality at work for the travelling photographer. For instance, Bourne and Shepherd[19], a photographic firm started by partners Samuel Bourne and Charles Shepherd "in search of

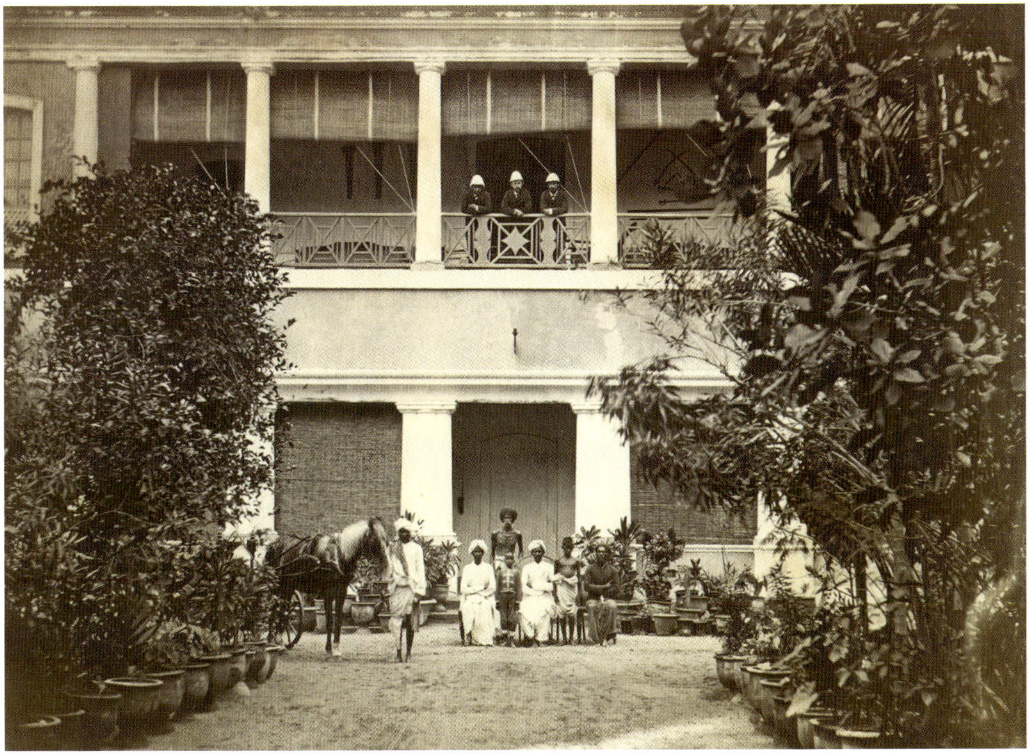

Facing page
Fig. 5
Unknown Photographer
Government House Pondichery,
c. 1880, Albumen Print, 150 x 217 mm
ACP: 97.48.0001(0041)

The Governor's House, located in the Government Square, was originally designed by Dumont, a French engineer, and was the residence of the French Governor Joseph-François Dupleix (1697-1763). Following the capture of Pondicherry by the British in 1761, the Governor's House was reconstructed on a more modest scale by Bouçet, another French engineer. At present, it is the residence of the Indian Lieutenant Governor, and is called "Raj Nivas".

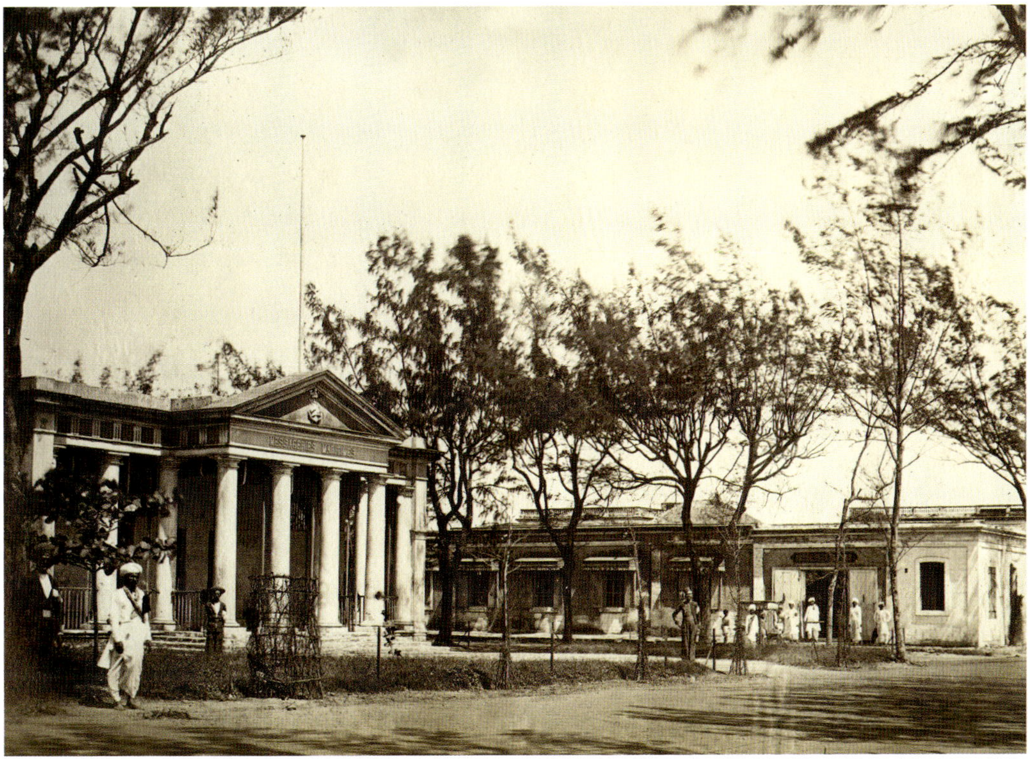

Above
Fig. 6
Unknown Photographer
Pondicherry: Living Quarters of the Textile Firm "Savanah," c. 1870
Albumen Print, 164 x 219 mm
ACP: 96.20.0154

Below
Fig. 7
Unknown Photographer
Messageries Maritimes (Post Office)-Pondichery, c. 1880
Albumen Print, 158 x 220 mm
ACP: 97.48.0001(0042)

The Messageries Maritimes was founded in 1851. Initially known as Messageries Nationales, then Messageries Impériales, it became Compagnie des Messageries Maritimes in 1871. The company was responsible for transporting passengers and goods between France and its colonies, as well as mail and messages.

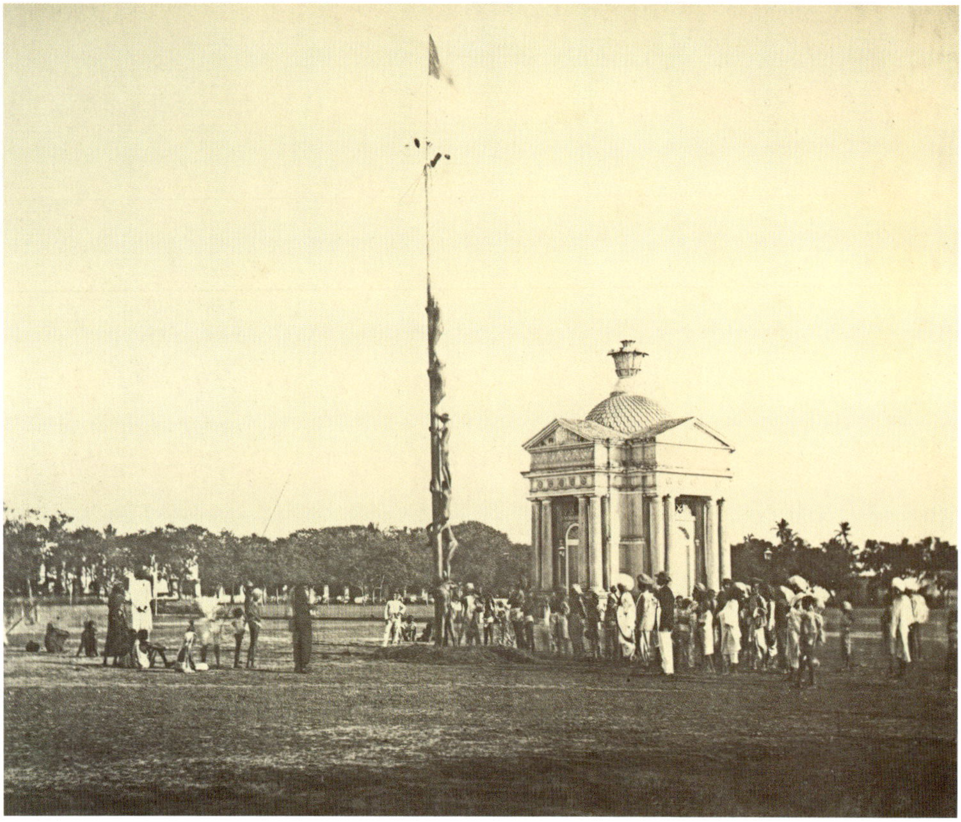

Fig. 8
C. (possibly Charles) Moyne
Fontaine de Pondichery (Fountain of Pondicherry famously known as, Aayi Mandapam), c. 1860, Albumen Print, 184 x 218 mm
ACP: 97.52.0001(0027)

The Government Square Fountain, also known as the 'Aayi Mandapam', stands within the Government Park. Built in Greco-Roman style, it housed a drinking water fountain. Envisaged by an engineer named Spinasse in 1820, the building got sanctioned by Governor Verninac and was finally completed in 1863 by another engineer, Lamairesse. Water was supplied to the town through a canal from a tank. However, according to a local legend this monument is named after a lady courtesan named Aayi. A king passing the residence of Aayi, mistook her home for a holy shrine. The king's misjudgment touched Aayi, who decided to replace her home with a reservoir. Affected by her gesture, Napoléon allegedly decided to erect a monument as a tribute to Aayi.

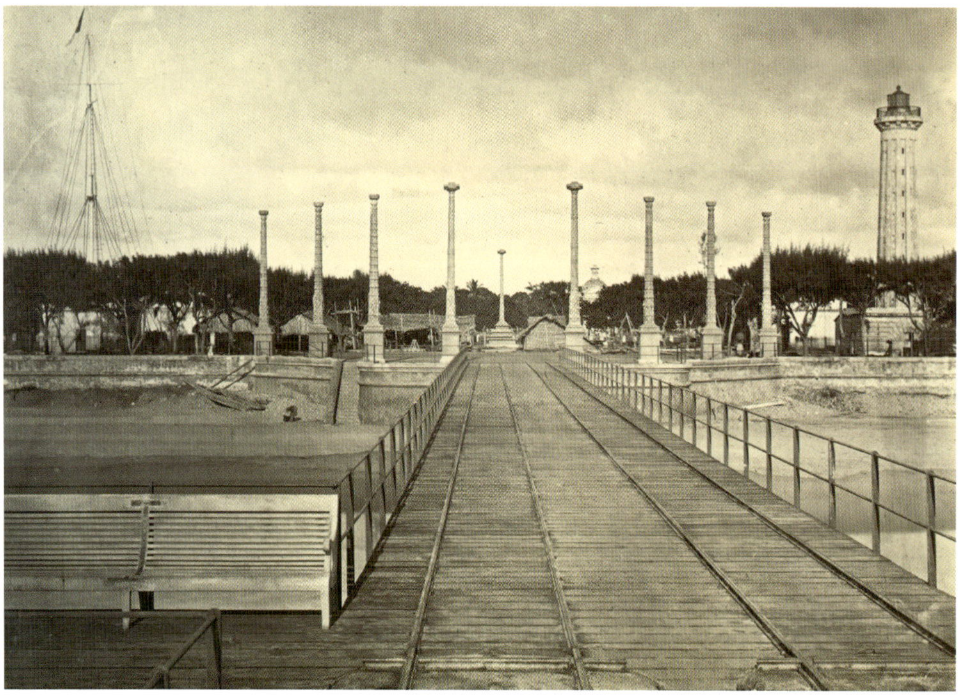

Fig. 9
C. (possibly Charles) Moyne
Port de Pondichery (Pondicherry, Gingee Fort Pillars and Light House), c. 1860, Albumen Print, 166 x 230 mm
ACP: 97.52.0001(0030)

The exquisitely carved monolithic pillars were brought to Pondicherry from the nearby Gingee Fort, after its capture in 1751. The pier was destroyed by a cyclone in 1952. Remnants of the two Decauville railway lines leading to the Republic Square can be noticed on the left and right of the pier.

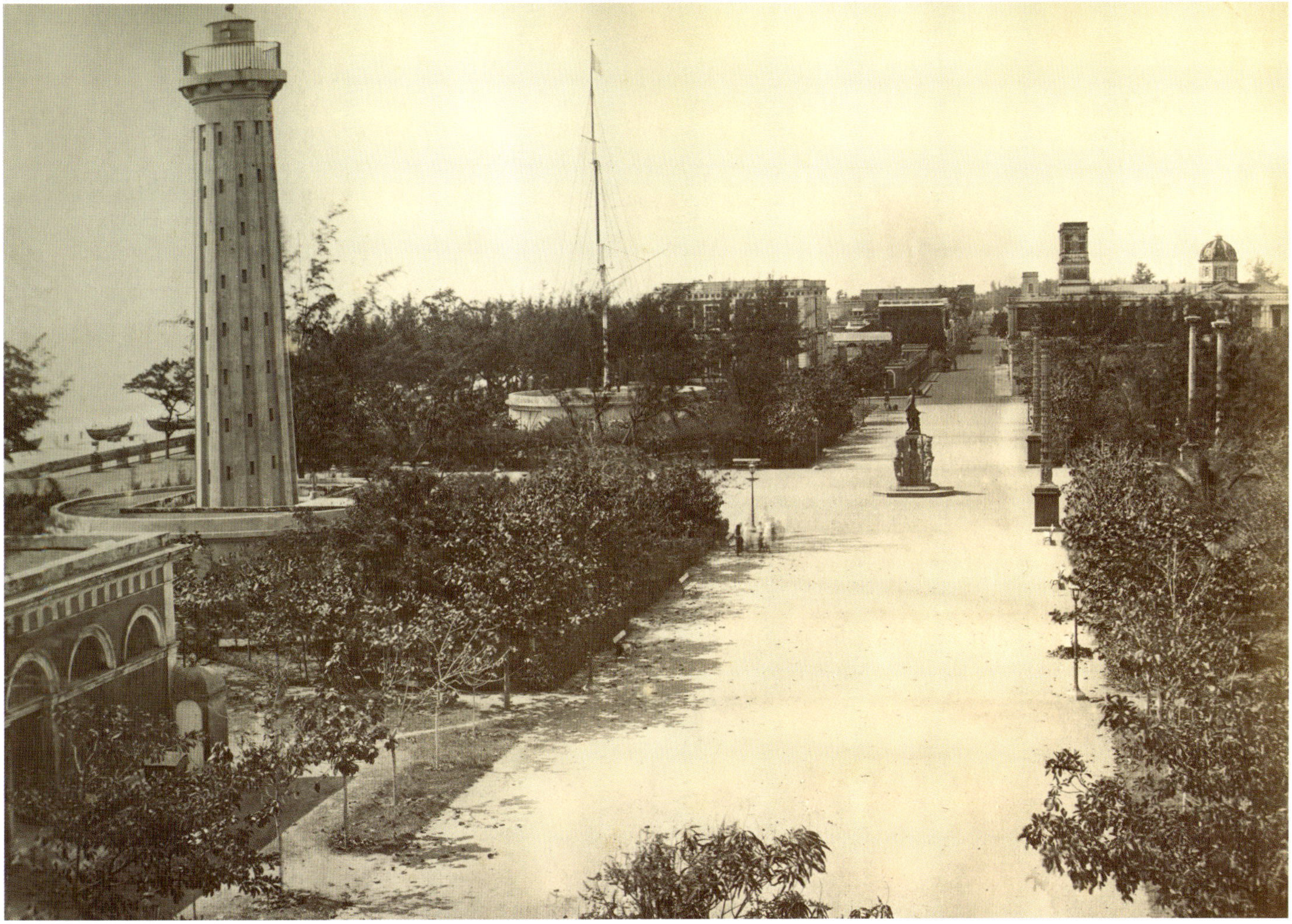

the picturesque",[20] produced a pageant of dramatic landscapes, noble monuments and romantic ruins,[21] capturing the colonial harbour town. The success of Bourne and Shepherd at the time was not only a product of their technical skill and commercial acumen but also their ability to present a vision of India that coincided with, and reinforced, colonial notions of the 'exotic' East.[22] With its agencies in Bombay, Calcutta and Simla as well as outlets in London and Paris (which included running a mail order system), this studio found ways to publicise and sell images of Pondicherry in the mid-1860s [Fig 11 & 12].

Aesthetically, the commanding style of that period was in the format of landscape photography or in this case, cityscapes, a dominant academic genre that gradually developed in 19th century Europe. Technically speaking, a lateral rectangular frame would be typically composed with a width greater than the height, compositionally following the 'golden rule' of one-third/two-third horizontal proportions. The landscape

Fig. 10
Unknown Photographer
Light House Pondichery in Public Gardens, c. 1880,
Albumen Print, 161 x 225 mm
ACP: 97.48.0001(0047)

The foundation stone of the lighthouse was laid in 1835 by Louis Guerre (project engineer) during Governor Saint-Simon's tenure. Standing 29 meters high, it cost about 10,000 Francs. When in operation, its light could allegedly be seen from a distance of 15 miles.

Some changes were incorporated in the building: a round base was built encircling the older square base; the first floor was added in the early 20th century; electric lights were added in 1913 and 1931, respectively.

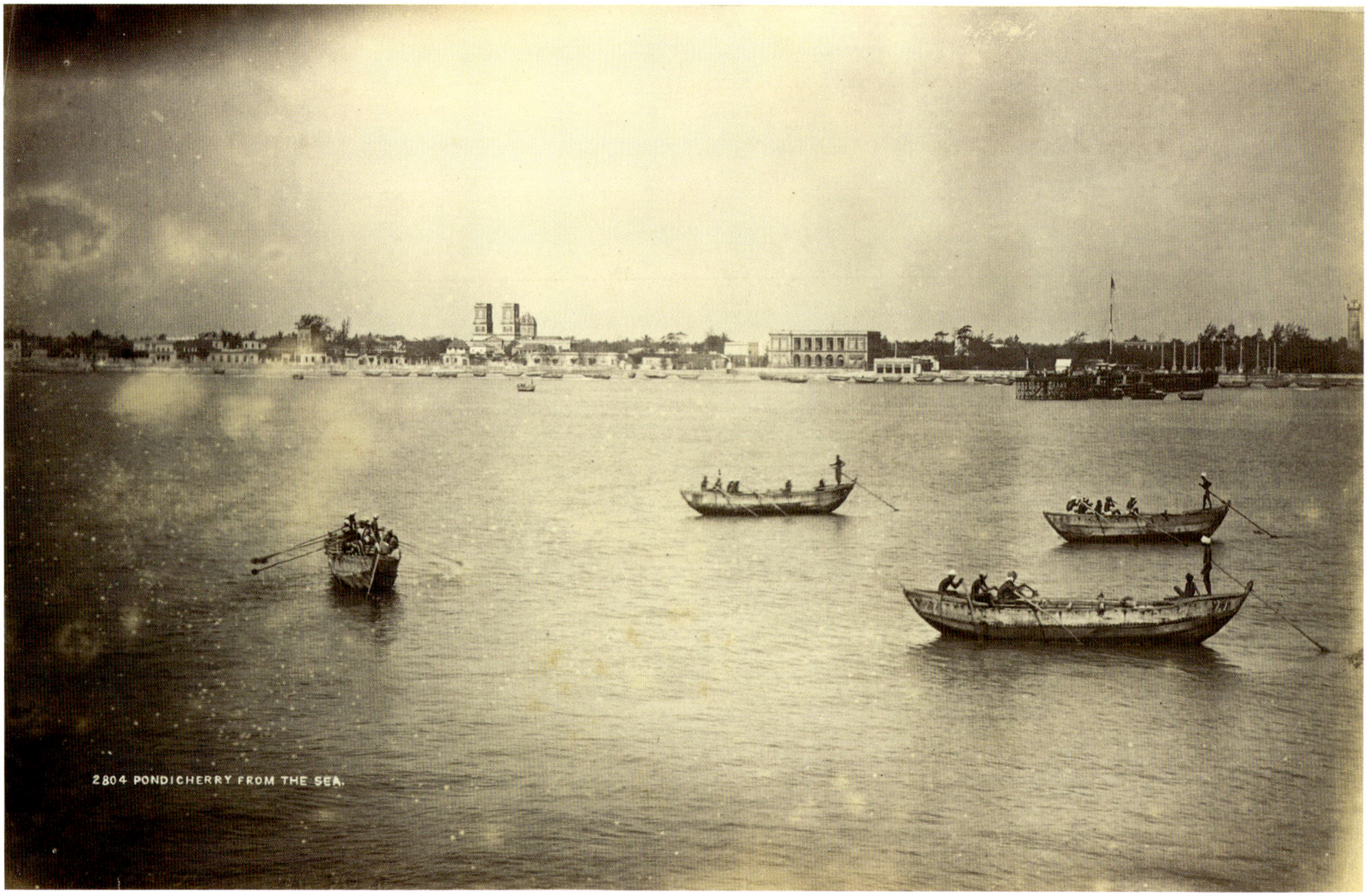

Fig. 11
Bourne & Shepherd
Pondicherry from the Sea, c. 1890,
Albumen Print, Photographer's Ref. 2804,
183 x 290 mm
ACP: 95.0015(0001)

A view of the "South Beach" in Pondicherry showing *chelingues*. The *chelingues* were sewed boats that could resist the waves of the Coromandel. Without a natural harbour and until the construction of the pier, these boats were the only means to carry goods and people from the ships to the shore.

Facing page
Fig. 12
Bourne & Shepherd
Railka: Pondicherry. Pondicherry, the 'push-push', a street conveyance, c. 1890,
Albumen Print, Photographer's Ref. 2808,
161 x 211 mm
ACP: 94.111.0019

This vehicle, also known as "La Pondichérienne" was the typical Pondicherian rickshaw. It was a four-wheeled covered cart pulled by two men and steered by the passengers. This mode of transport was possibly confined to this French colony.

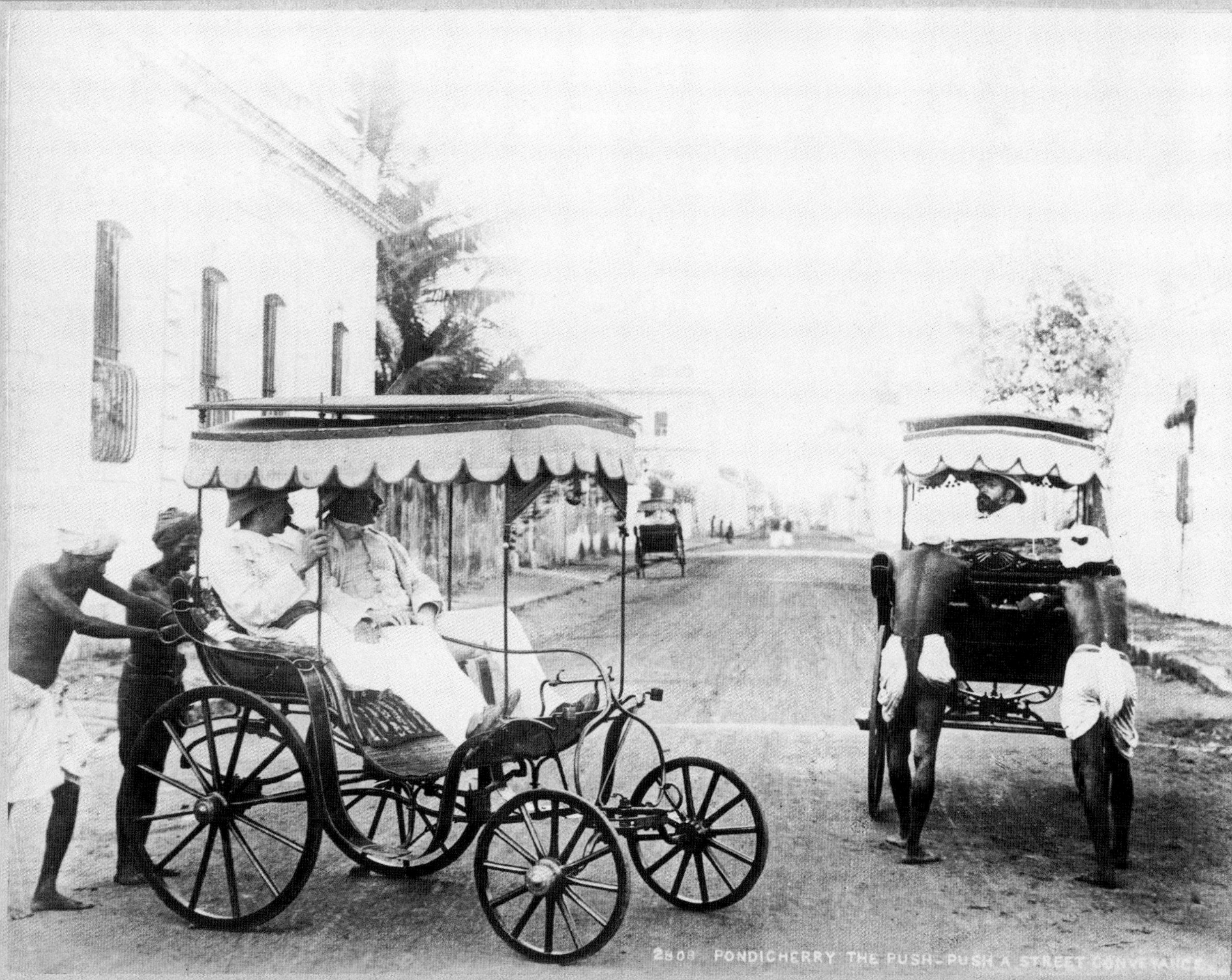

Railka : Pondicherry ...

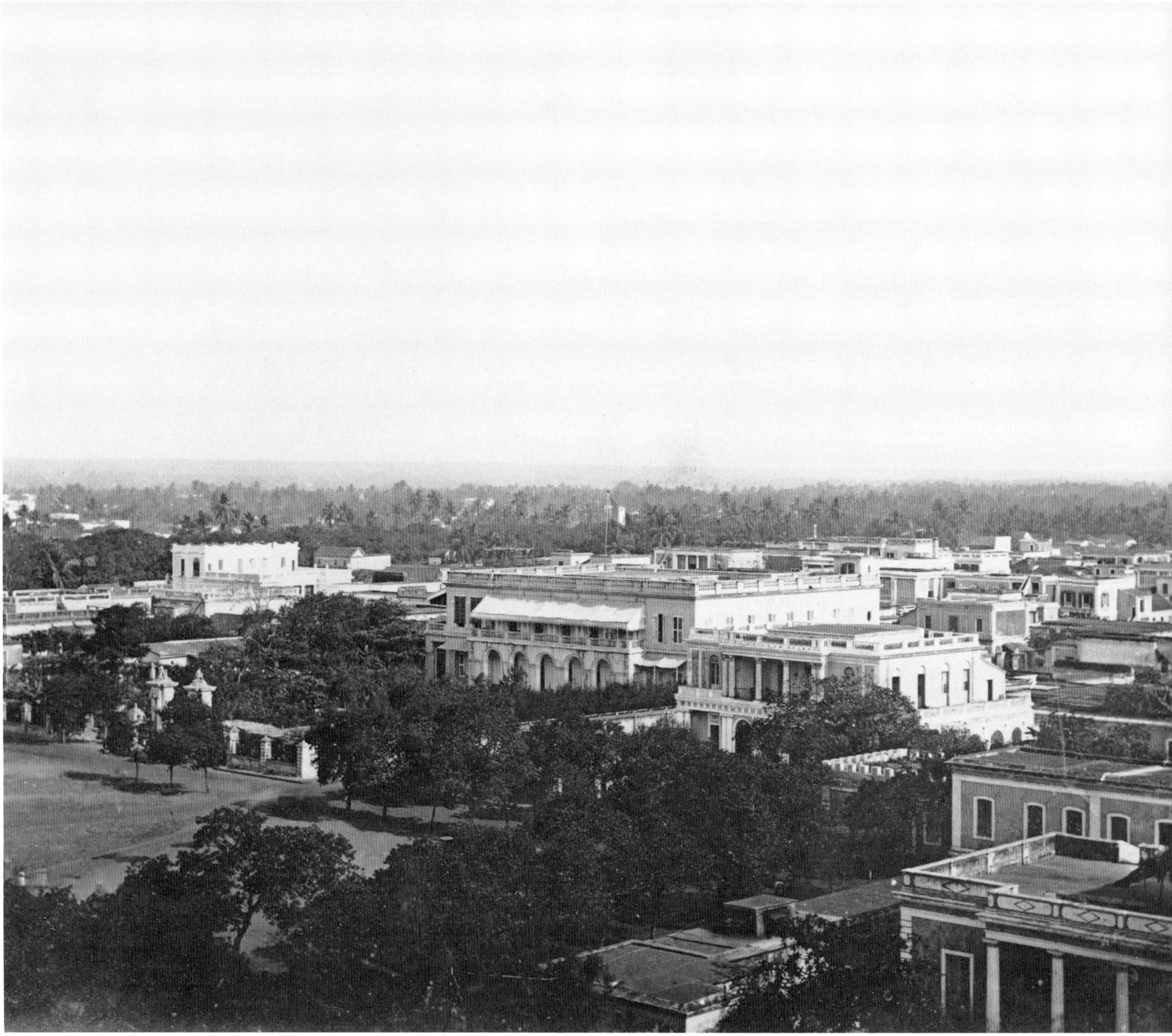

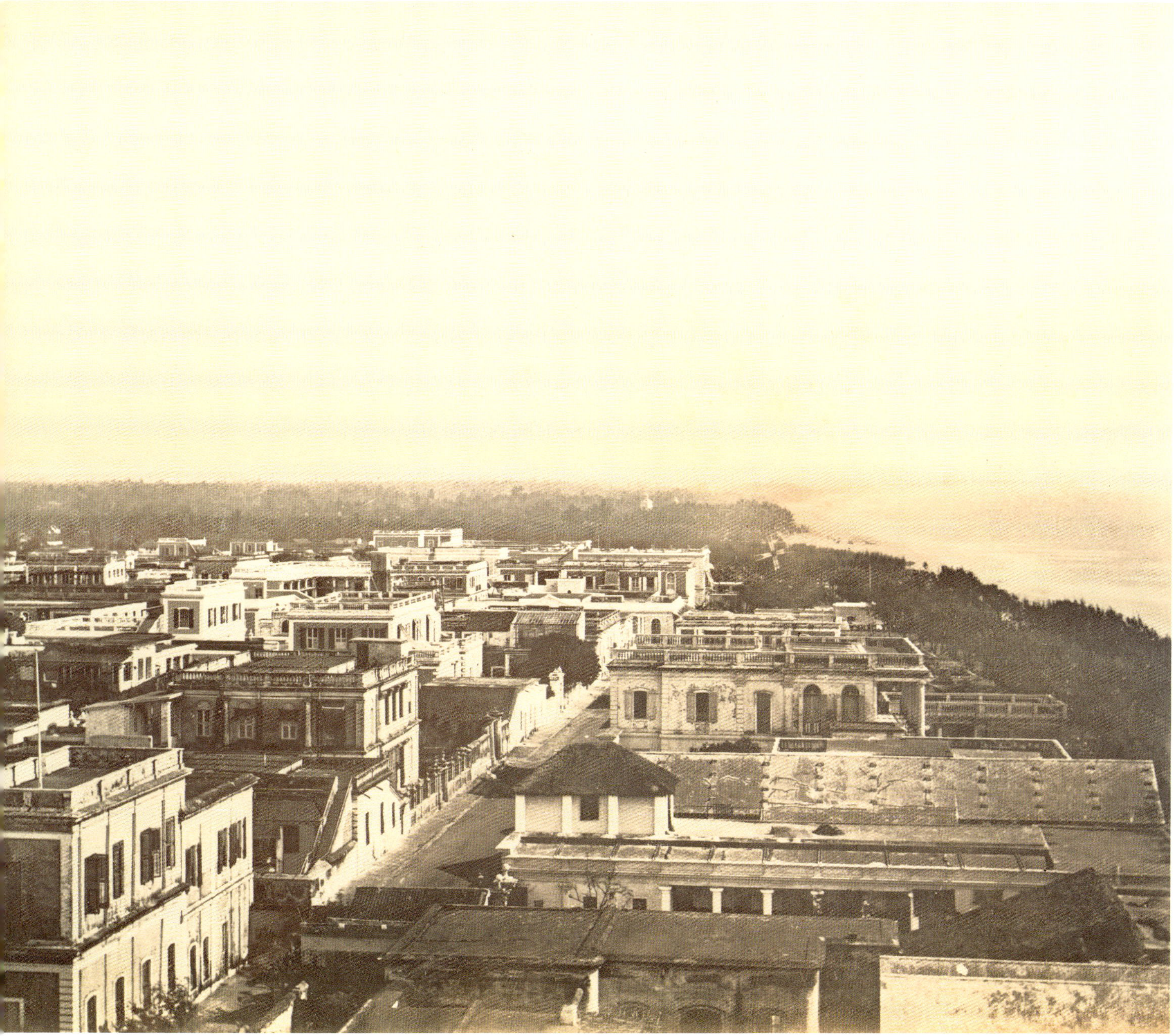

Fig. 13
C. (possibly Charles) Moyne
General [Panoramic] View of
Pondicherry, c. 1860
Albumen Print, 188 x 456 mm
ACP: 97.52.0001(0028 & 0029)

then appeared as an antidote for the visual and social consequences of industrialisation, offering a therapeutic view of the city, as a pastoral sensibility emerging out of commerce and industry.[23]

Another photographer (allegedly French), working in South India in the 1860s was C. (possibly Charles) Moyne. Applying the tenet of architectural photography—the use of controlled perspective, with an emphasis on vertical lines that are non-converging (parallel), he actively photographed the landscapes and monuments of Pondicherry in this period.[24] Unlike a studio photographer who could control the demeanour of the subject, an architectural photographer was technically constrained, challenged not only by natural elements, but also by having to develop his negatives on the spot, often using combustible chemicals such as potassium iodide and silver nitrate. The photographs present vistas with an all-encapsulating sense of the city seen from a vantage point [Fig 13 & 14].

Such architectural images abound in the archive of 19th century photographs in India which also include the work of other photo-graphers in the South Indian region such as Nicholas and Company, Alexander Greenlaw and Linnaeus Tripe , based out of Madras; or travelling photographers such as A.T.W. Penn who captured the famine affected people of Madras. The Madras School of Arts was established in 1850 by Dr. Alexander Hunter who introduced photography for students with Lineaus Tripe (who eventually became famous for his views of Burma) providing tuitions.[25] The aim of such an exercise was to train a group of individuals who could be incorporated in the government's surveying and docu-mentary activities. Photography's qualities as an instructive pastime, combining potential for artistic expression with the practical merits of information gathering, were often discussed in these societies. Official encouragement of, and tuition in, photography from the mid-1850s resulted in impressive work produced by officers who had taken up photography as a hobby or profession.

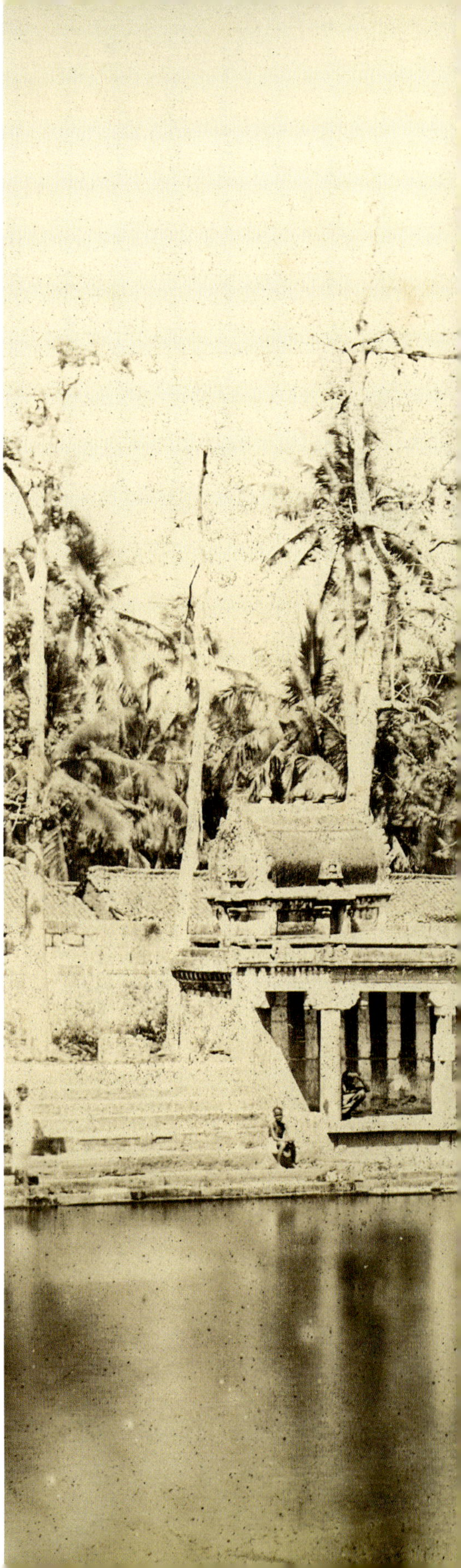

Fig. 14
C. (possibly Charles) Moyne
c. 1860, Albumen Print, 162 x 216 mm
ACP: 2008.01.0046

48. Pagode de Vilnour, Cour Interieure, Etang Sacre. Environs de Pondichery. (Pagoda Vilnour, Inner Court, Sacred Tank, Around Pondicherry-Gokilambal Thirukameshwar Temple, Sacred Tank.)

The Sri Gokilambal Thirukameshwar Temple is located 10 km away from Pondicherry, in Villianur. The temple dates back to the Chola period (12th century) and is dedicated to Shiva.

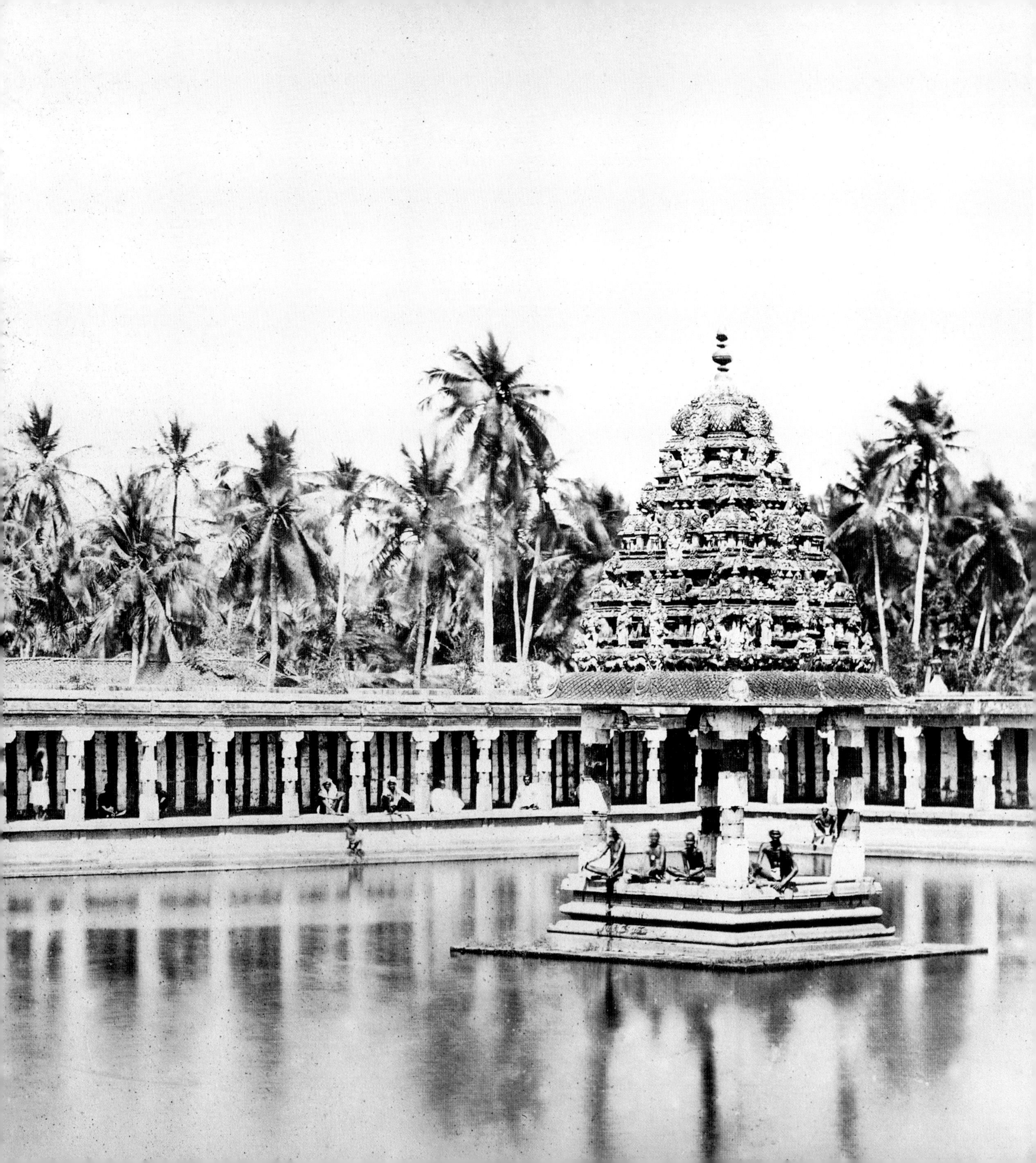

HISTORICISING THE ALBUM
SRI AUROBINDO AND HIS ASHRAM

Looking at albums redoubles the storytelling impulse that photographs naturally trigger.

Verna Posever Curtis[26]

From their earliest days, albums have been made for preserving impressions and recreating memories. The photographic album presents a unique, and multi-faceted sub-genre within the history of photography, which began in the mid 19th century and flourished with the technical expansion of photography during the 20th century. The commercial production of albums—paper, binding, and covers—were representations of the compiler's aesthetic sensibility.[27] The *Sri Aurobindo And His Ashram* album in The Alkazi Collection of Photography is a collection of 119 black and white photographs in 48 folios bound in original brocade cloth without tilting. Interestingly, the cover folio has a cloth-embroidered image of Srinathji, that form of Krishna when he lifted the Govardhan Parvat (hill) on his little finger, from Nathdwara in Rajasthan [Fig 15].

The images in the album comprise those of Sri Aurobindo as well as the Mother. Sri Aurobindo Ghosh's (1872–1950) 'image' and teachings in India were popularised in Europe, leading to his nomination for the Nobel Prize in 1950. This event stirred an interest in his intellectual persona internationally. Brought up and educated in Cambridge (England) Sri Aurobindo joined the fight for India's independence when he came back to India. His activities greatly influenced the outward predilections of Gandhi and Nehru's non-violent, peaceful measures of political conduct.[28] In 1910, he withdrew from politics and retired to Pondicherry in order to devote himself entirely to his inner spiritual life and work. During his 40 years in Pondicherry, he evolved a new method of spiritual practice, which he called the Integral Yoga. Eventually, in 1926, with the help of his spiritual collaborator, the Mother, he founded the Sri Aurobindo Ashram.[29]

The Mother, Sri Aurobindo Ghosh's divine companion, a French Jewess by birth, was born as Mirra Alfassa (1878–1973) in Paris.

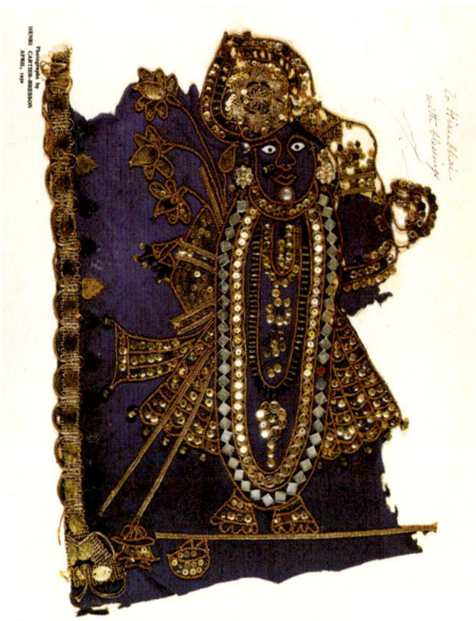

Fig. 15
Srinathji–Frontend paper from the album 'Sri Aurobindo and His Ashram', c. 1950
Sequins and Zari on Indigo dyed Cotton Cloth pasted on paper, 403 x 315 mm
ACP: D2005.06.0001

An accomplished artist, she studied at *Ecole Des Beaux Arts* (Paris) and excelled as a pianist and writer. Interested in occultism, she visited Tlemcen (Algeria) in 1905 and 1906 to study with the adept spiritualist Max Theon and his wife. Her primary interest, however, was in the spiritual development of humanity. In Paris, she founded a group of spiritual seekers and gave talks to various groups, before arriving in India in 1914, when she visited Pondicherry to meet Sri Aurobindo. After a stay of 11 months she was obliged to return to France due to the outbreak of the World War I. A year later she went to Japan for a period of four years. Finally, in April 1920, the Mother rejoined Sri Aurobindo in Pondicherry. When Sri Aurobindo Ashram was formed in November 1926, Sri Aurobindo entrusted its full material and spiritual charge to the Mother. Under her guidance, which continued for nearly 50 years, the Ashram grew into a large artists' complex. In 1952 she established Sri Aurobindo International Centre of Education, and in 1968 an international township, Auroville.[30]

Four times a year, Sri Aurobindo appeared before his devotees from all parts of Bengal, Gujarat and elsewhere, seen in some of the photographs featured in the album. The disciples of the Ashram paraded in formation (the colour of their shorts indicate the degree of physical training completed) winding up in the room where Aurobindo and the Mother sat side by side, at *darshan*,[31] a period during which the disciples came to commune with the holy spirit embodied in Aurobindo and the Mother. For hours the faithful would pass in front of them—the Mother dressed in long veils of gold covering her forehead down to the eyebrows and Aurobindo like an old seer, ornamented with silk; their feet rested on a tiger skin, where the disciples placed their flowers.[32] Ever since he withdrew to Pondicherry, Aurobindo Ghosh was rarely photographed. The Ashram currently has about10 portraits shot between 1910-26.[33] Several of them show him posing in front of artificial back-drops. The last of these pictures seem to have been taken during the early or middle 1920s by an anonymous photographer. In 1926 Sri Aurobindo retired and no photographs of him were taken for a quarter of a century. Copies of the earlier photographs were given to devotees, some of whom commented that the Sri Aurobindo they saw at *darshan* looked "quite different" from his pictures.[34]

CARTIER-BRESSON'S PHOTOGRAPHIC INTERVENTION

Some months after founding Magnum Photos with Robert Capa, Werner Biscoe, David Seymour, Ernst Haas and George Rodger, Henri Cartier-Bresson came to the East. His photographs of Gandhi's funeral in January 1948 won him an Overseas Press Club Award. On 13 April 1950, while he was in India, he wrote to the Sri Aurobindo Ashram from Madras.[35] His letter was addressed to the Ashram's Secretary General, Philippe Barbier Saint-Hilaire, known as Pavitra. Bresson was already known as one of the world's leading photographers in the Sri Aurobindo Ashram.[36]

Introducing himself as a professional photographer associated with Magnum Photos, Cartier-Bresson asked for permission to attend the *darshan* of 24 April 1950 and to make a photographic reportage on the Ashram's life. The next day, 14 April, Cartier-Bresson was in Tiruvannamalai to see and photograph Bhagavan Ramana Maharshi. That very day at 8.47 pm in the evening, Sri Ramana attained Mahasamadhi. Cartier-Bresson was on hand to photograph his funeral. Returning to Madras he found a reply to his letter to the Ashram granting him permission to attend the *darshan* of the 24th and approving his request to make a photographic reportage on the Ashram's life. Cartier-Bresson arrived in Pondicherry on 23 April. According to his own account he was introduced to the Mother by Francois Baron, the Commissarie (formerly Governor) of Pondicherry, which was still a French possession.[37]

After a great deal of persuasion by the Mother, Sri Aurobindo agreed to be photo-graphed by Bresson [Figs 16, 17]. One condition, however, was set down by the Mother, that they be surrounded by an "Artistic Shadow", to reflect the atmosphere

Below
Fig. 16
Henri Cartier-Bresson
Sri Aurobindo Ghosh from the album 'Sri Aurobindo and His Ashram,' April 1950, Gelatin Silver Prints, 315 x 403 mm (each)
ACP: D2005.06.0001(0006-7)

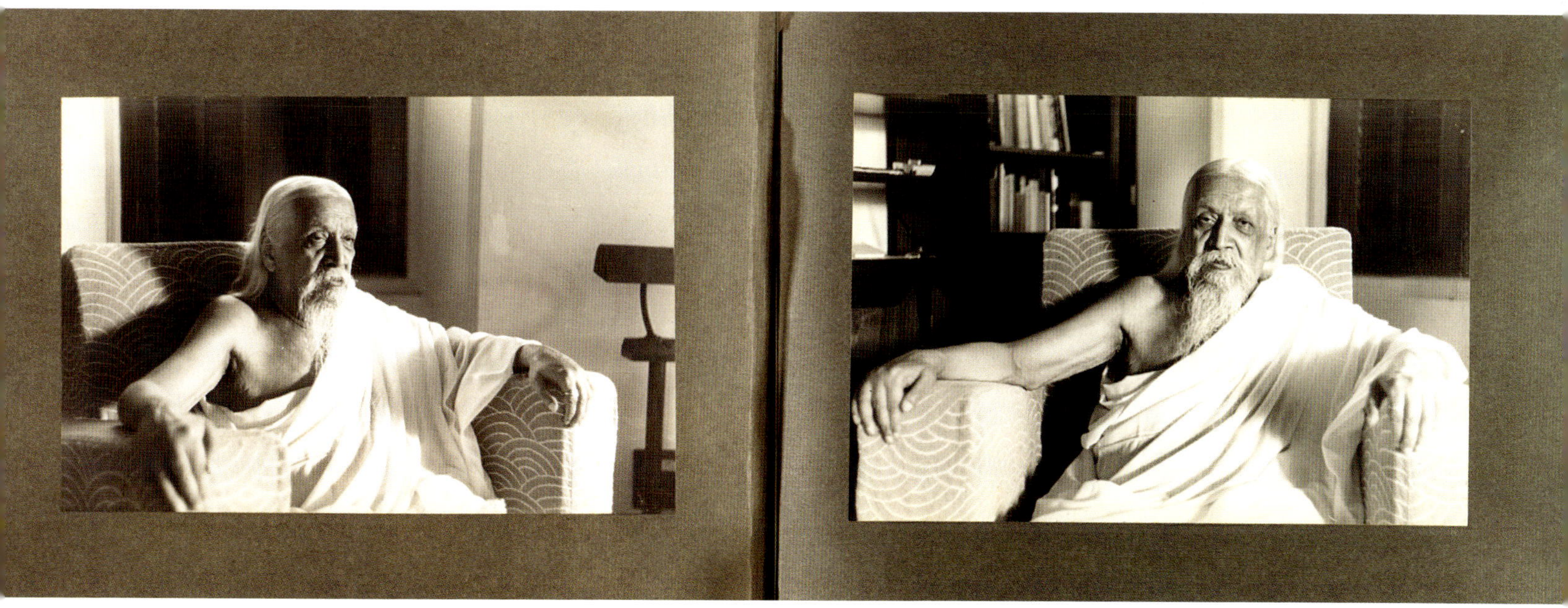

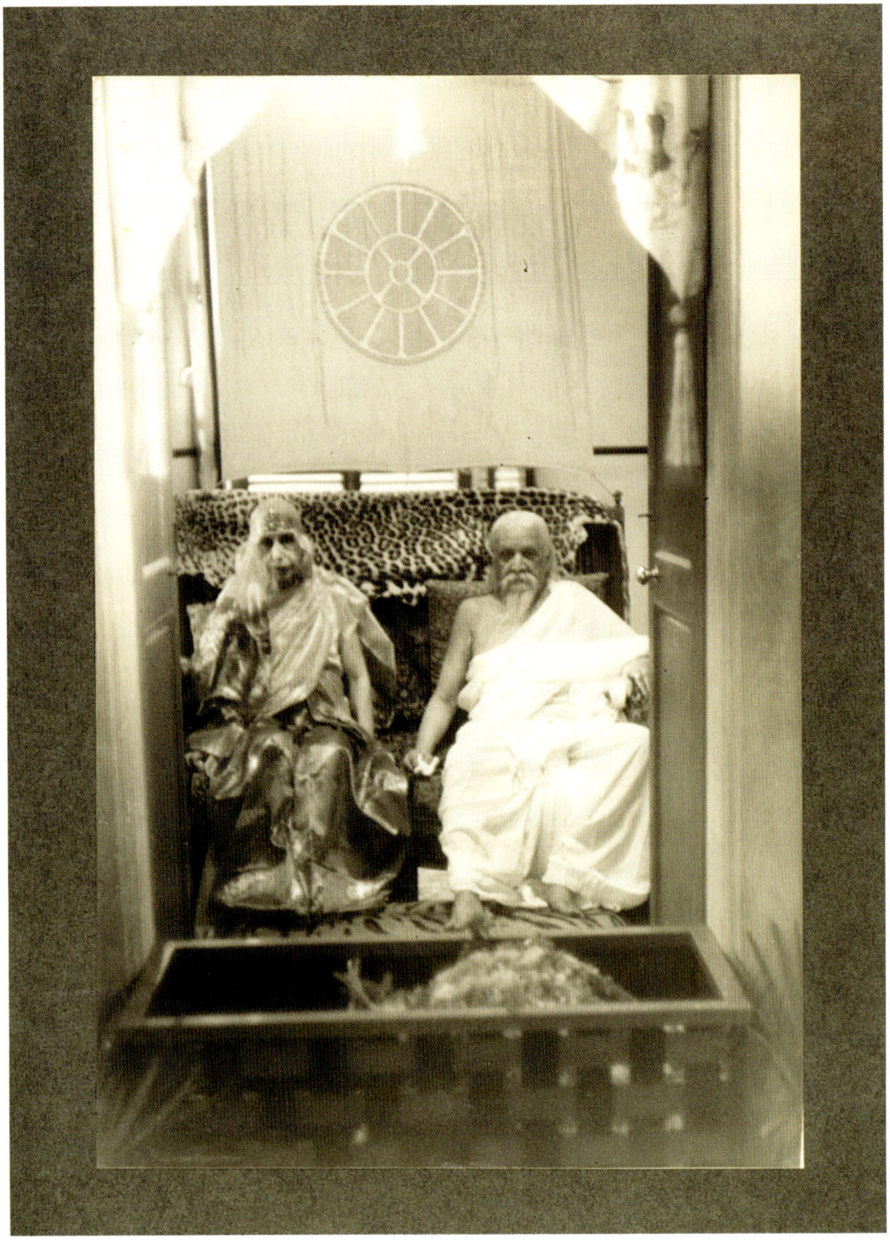

Fig. 17

Henri Cartier-Bresson

Sri Aurobindo Ghosh and The Mother at Darshan from the album 'Sri Aurobindo and His Ashram,' April 1950, Gelatin Silver Print, 403 x 315 mm

ACP: D2005.06.0001(0018)

Note 760-6 from Bresson's personal diary

'Four times a year Sri Aurobindo puts in an appearance before his disciples. They are allowed to file past him, one by one, and many deposit flowers in a hold at his feet. He sits immovable for hours, in a sort of tabernacle with silk ornament. Next to him is the Mother, his counterpart in divinity, in long gold veils covering her forehead down to the eyebrows and looking like a Byzantine Empress.'

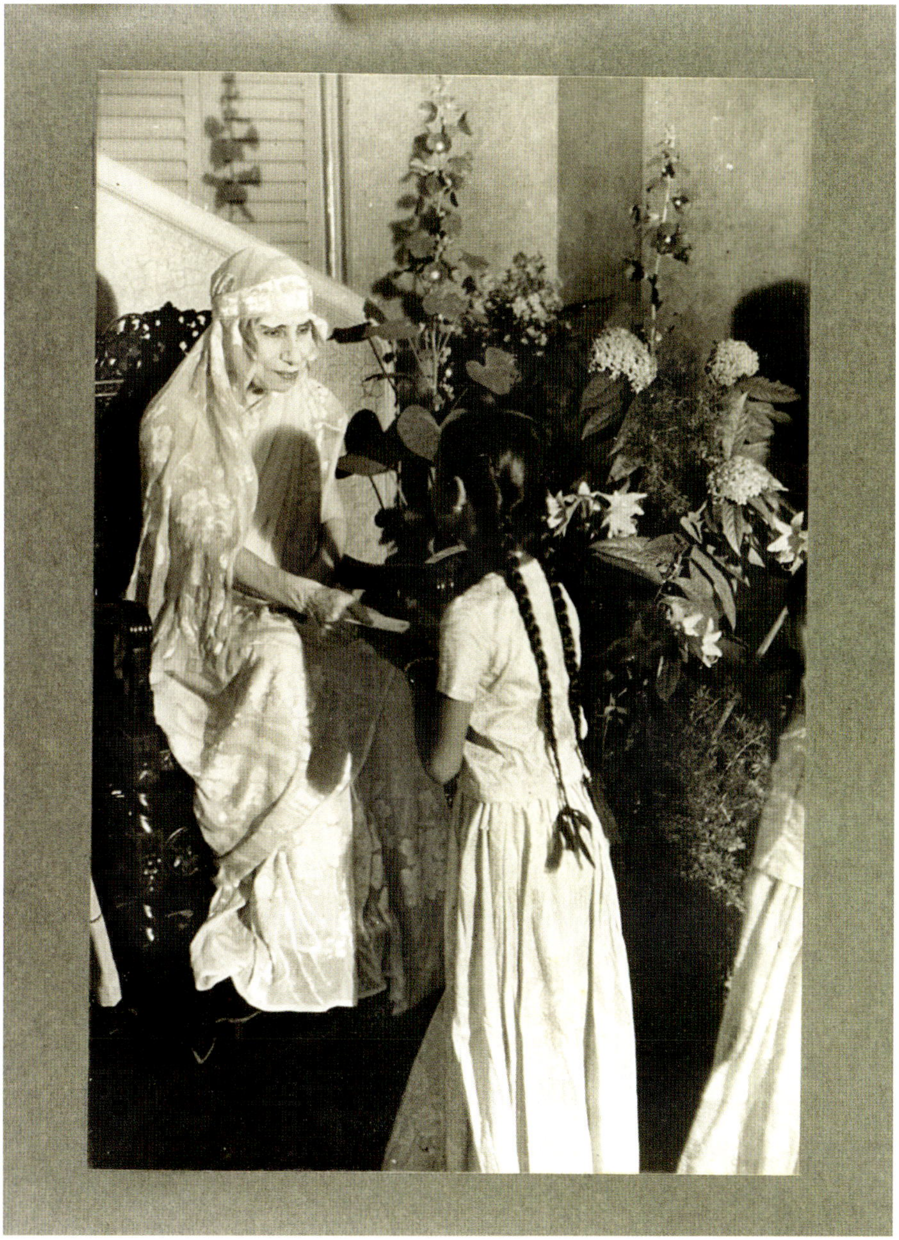

Fig. 18
Henri Cartier-Bresson
The Mother giving flowers to a child from the album 'Sri Aurobindo and His Ashram,' April 1950, Gelatin Silver Print, 403 x 315 mm
ACP: D2005.06.0001(0025)

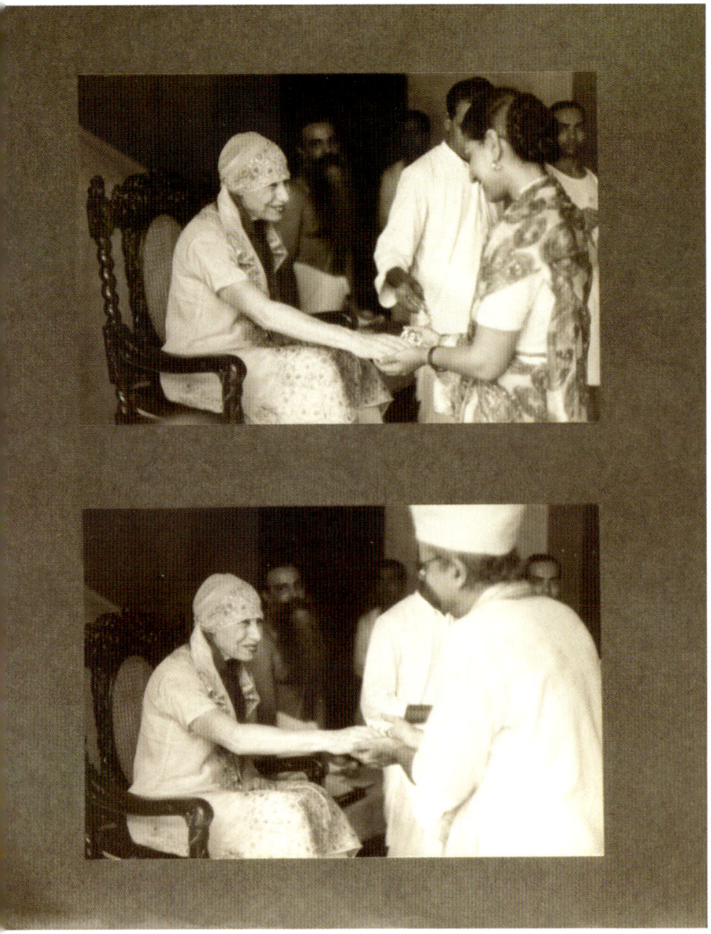

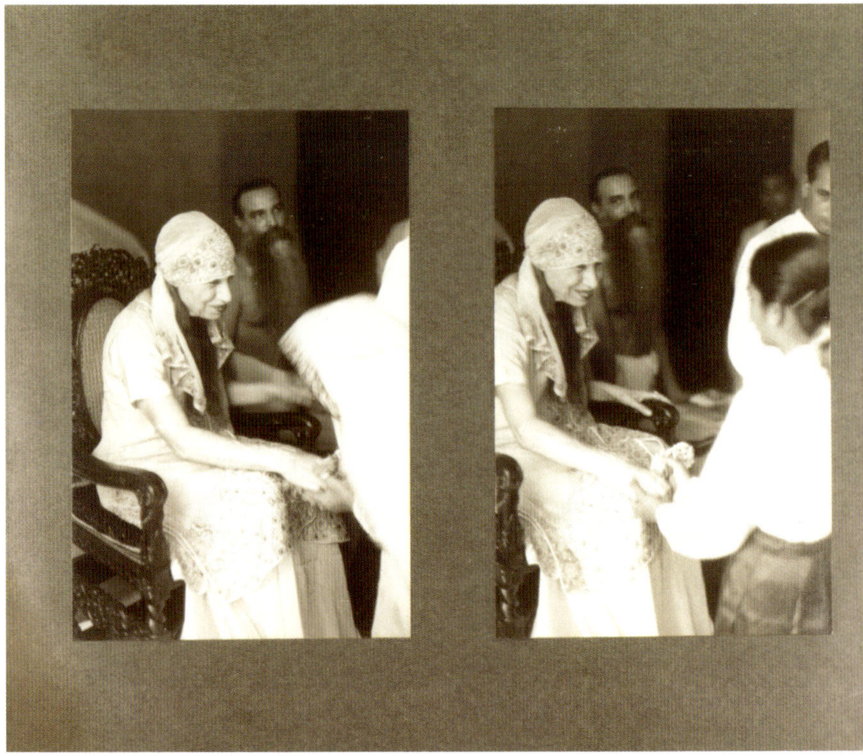

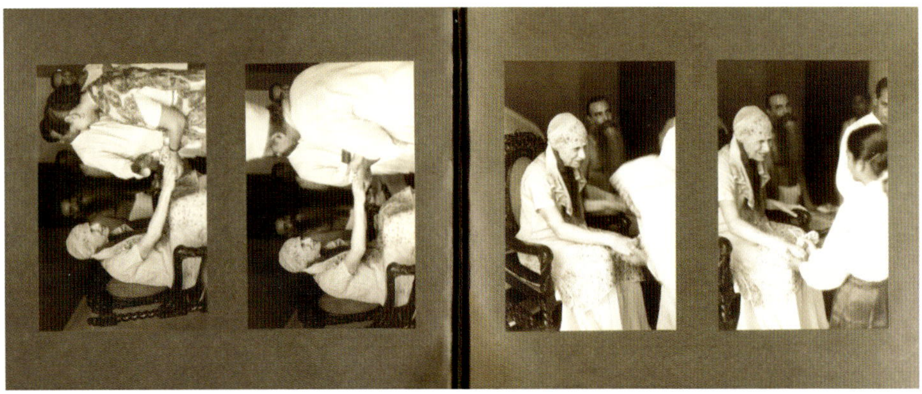

Left
Fig. 19
Henri Cartier-Bresson
The Mother at the daily ritual of receiving devotees from the album 'Sri Aurobindo and His Ashram,' April 1950, Gelatin Silver Prints, 403 x 315 mm (each)
ACP: D2005.06.0001(0032-35)

Above
Details of Fig. 19

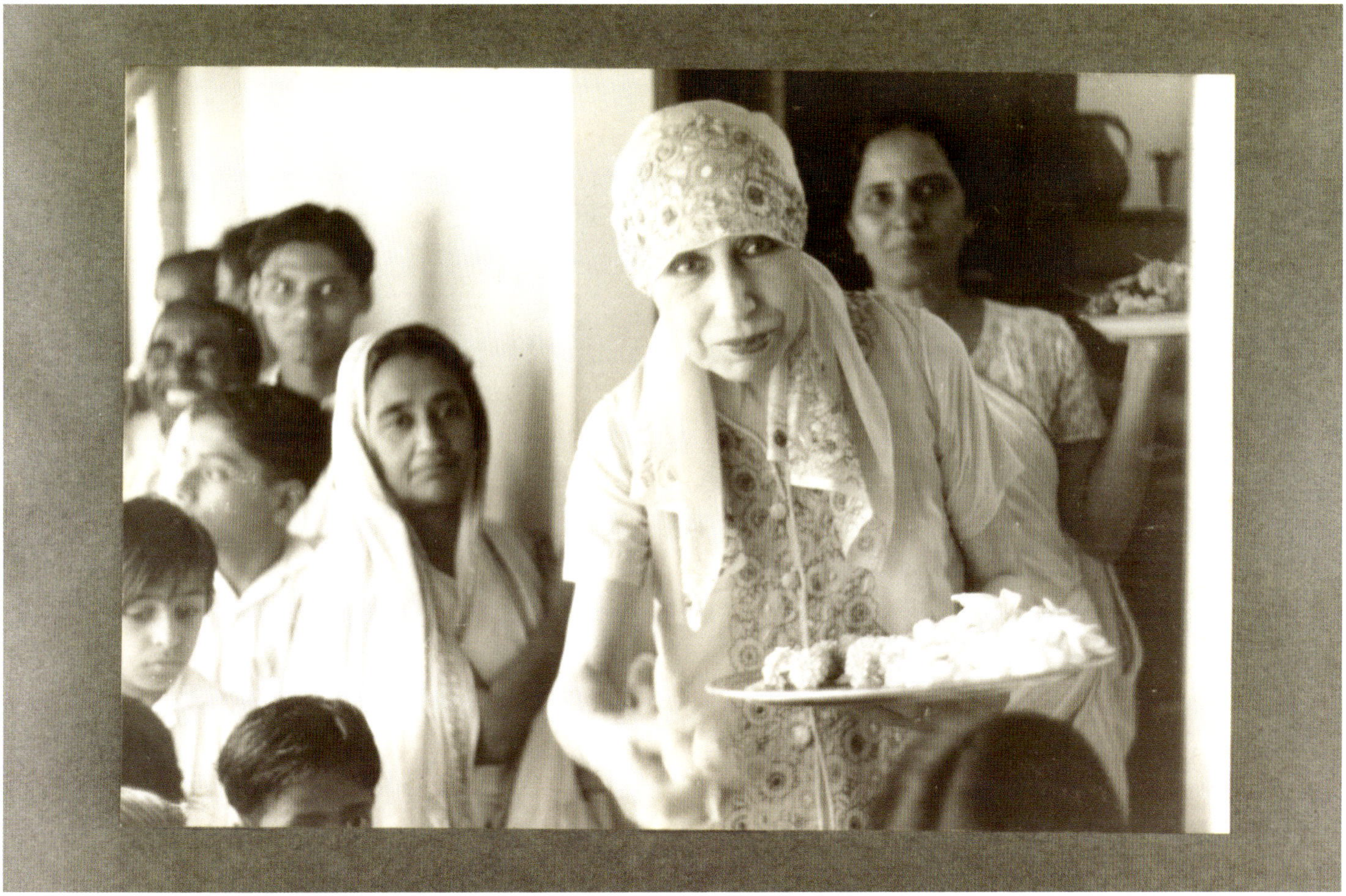

of this place of worship. In an audience with the Mother the following morning, Bresson firmly but gently explained that his photographs had so much artistic softness that not only would the pictures be a disappointment to the millions of faithful, but that his reputation as a portraitist was also at stake. The Mother finally allowed Cartier-Bresson to work in his own way. He had to promise, however, that he would submit all pictures for approval before publication.[38] Alongside photographing Sri Aurobindo, Bresson also captured the Mother [Figs 18, 19, 20, 21]. This album shot by Bresson of Sri Aurobindo, the Mother, the Ashram and its people turned out to be of significant importance not only to the devotees but also to documentary photography [Figs 22, 23, 24]. Apart from being captured by the lens after 30 years, Aurobindo Ghosh passed away 7 months after this photo-shoot.

The Ashram made 50 copies of the Album containing a selection of these photos, signed by the Mother.[39] The Mother had purchased all the negatives and prints from Bresson paying the professional charges of $3000 to Magnum Photos Inc. in 1951.[40]

Fig. 20
Henri Cartier-Bresson
[The Mother at the daily ritual of throwing flowers at the devotees] from the album 'Sri Aurobindo and His Ashram,' April 1950, Gelatin Silver Print, 315 x 403 mm
ACP: D2005.06.0001(0054)

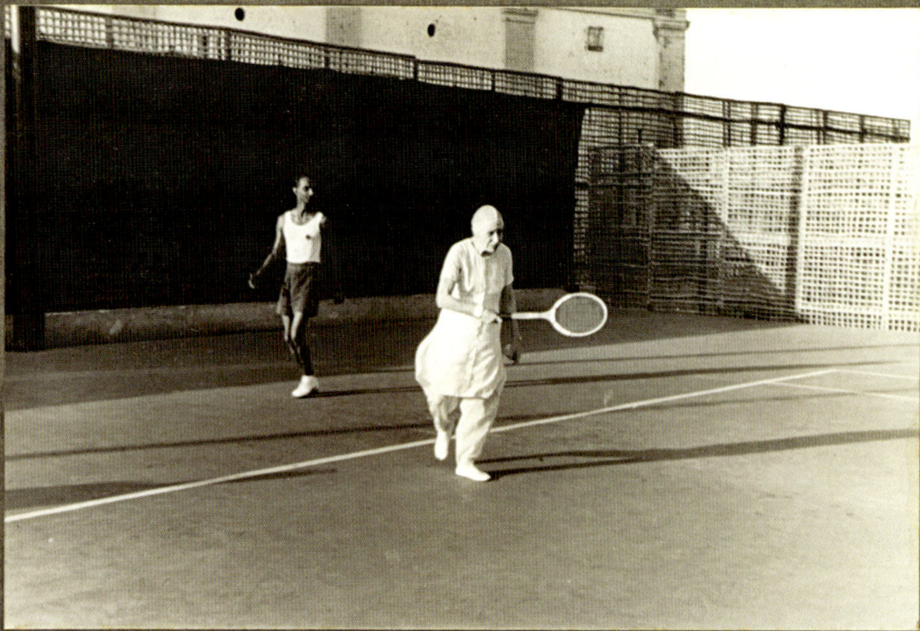

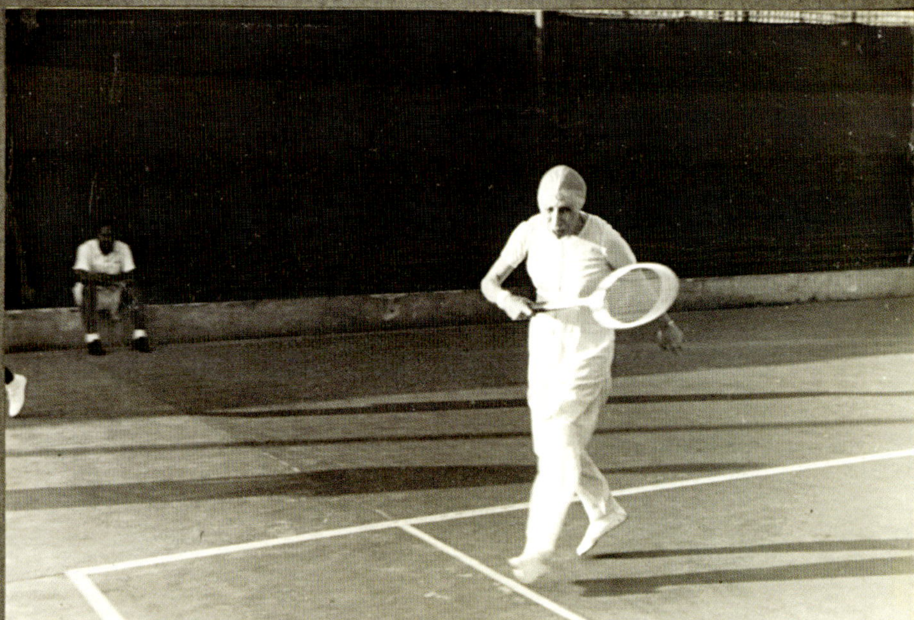

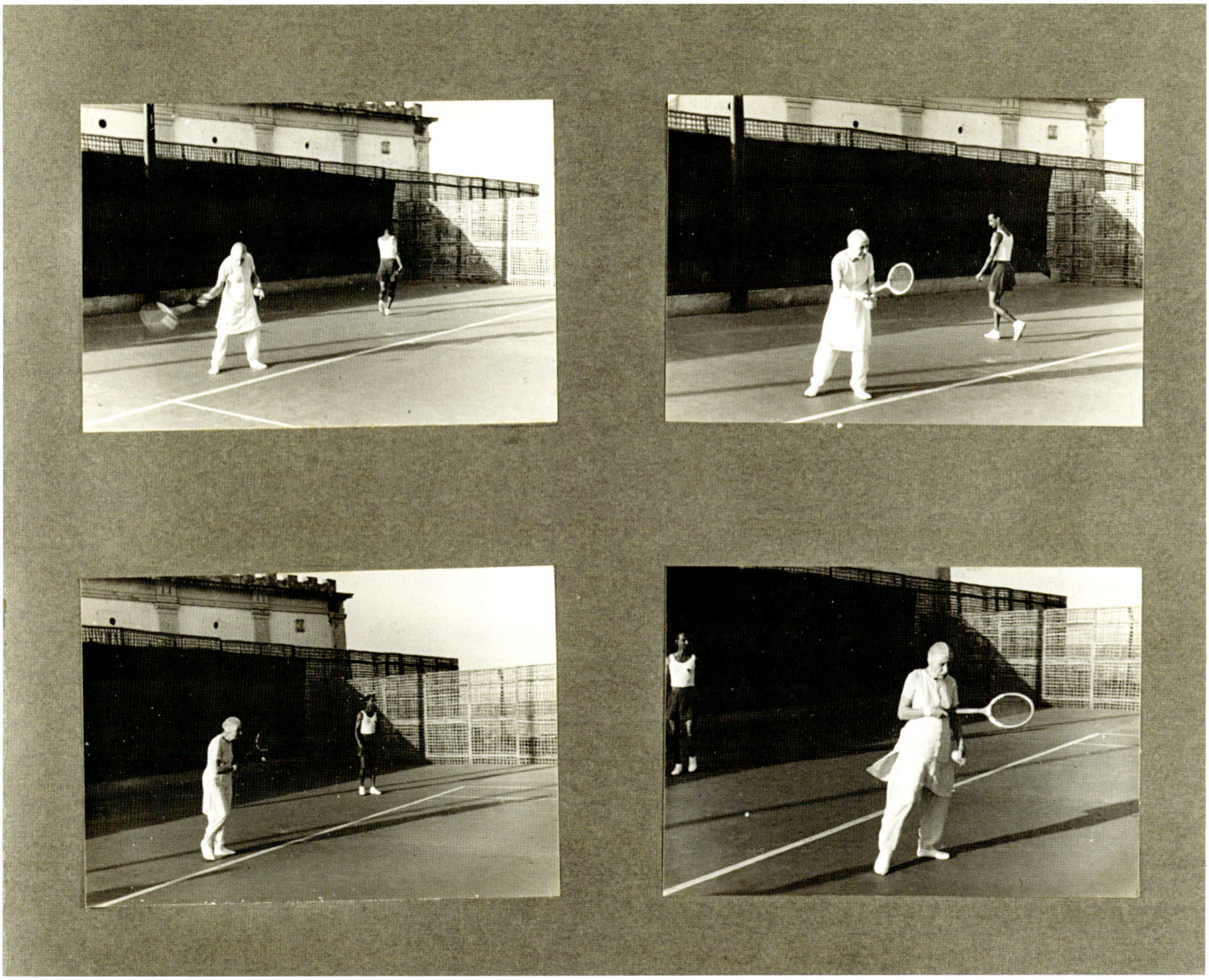

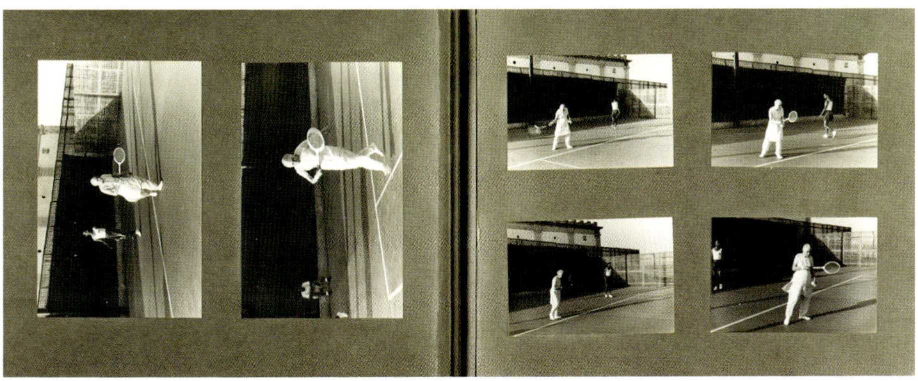

Left
Fig. 21
Henri Cartier-Bresson
[The Mother playing tennis] from the album 'Sri Aurobindo and His Ashram,' April 1950, Gelatin Silver Prints, 315 x 403 mm (each)
ACP: D2005.06.0001(0079-84)

Facing page and above
Details of Fig. 21

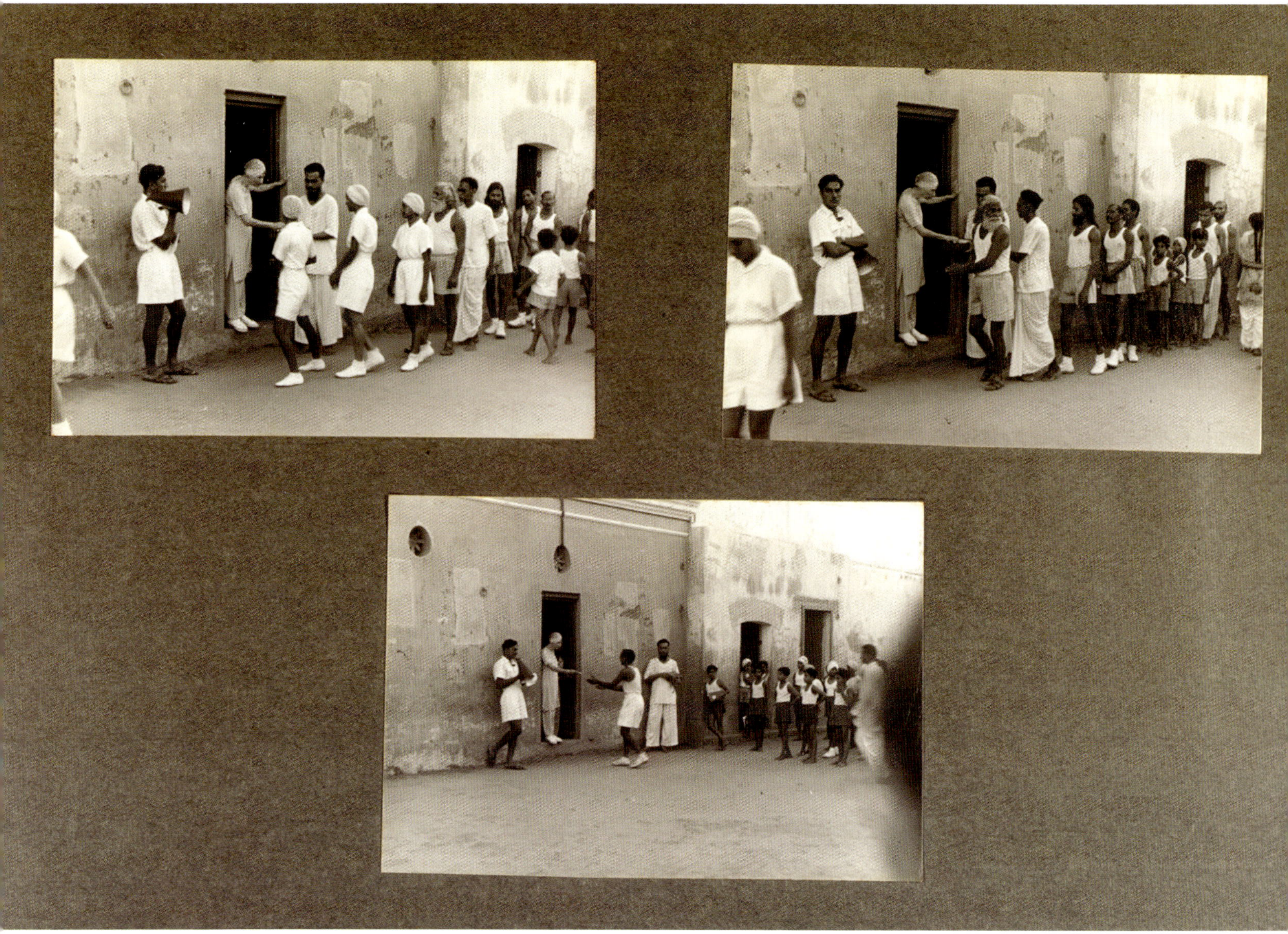

Fig. 22
Henri Cartier-Bresson
[Daily activities at the Ashram with the Mother]
from the album 'Sri Aurobindo and His Ashram,'
April 1950, Gelatin Silver Prints, 315 x 403 mm
ACP: D2005.06.0001(0094-96)

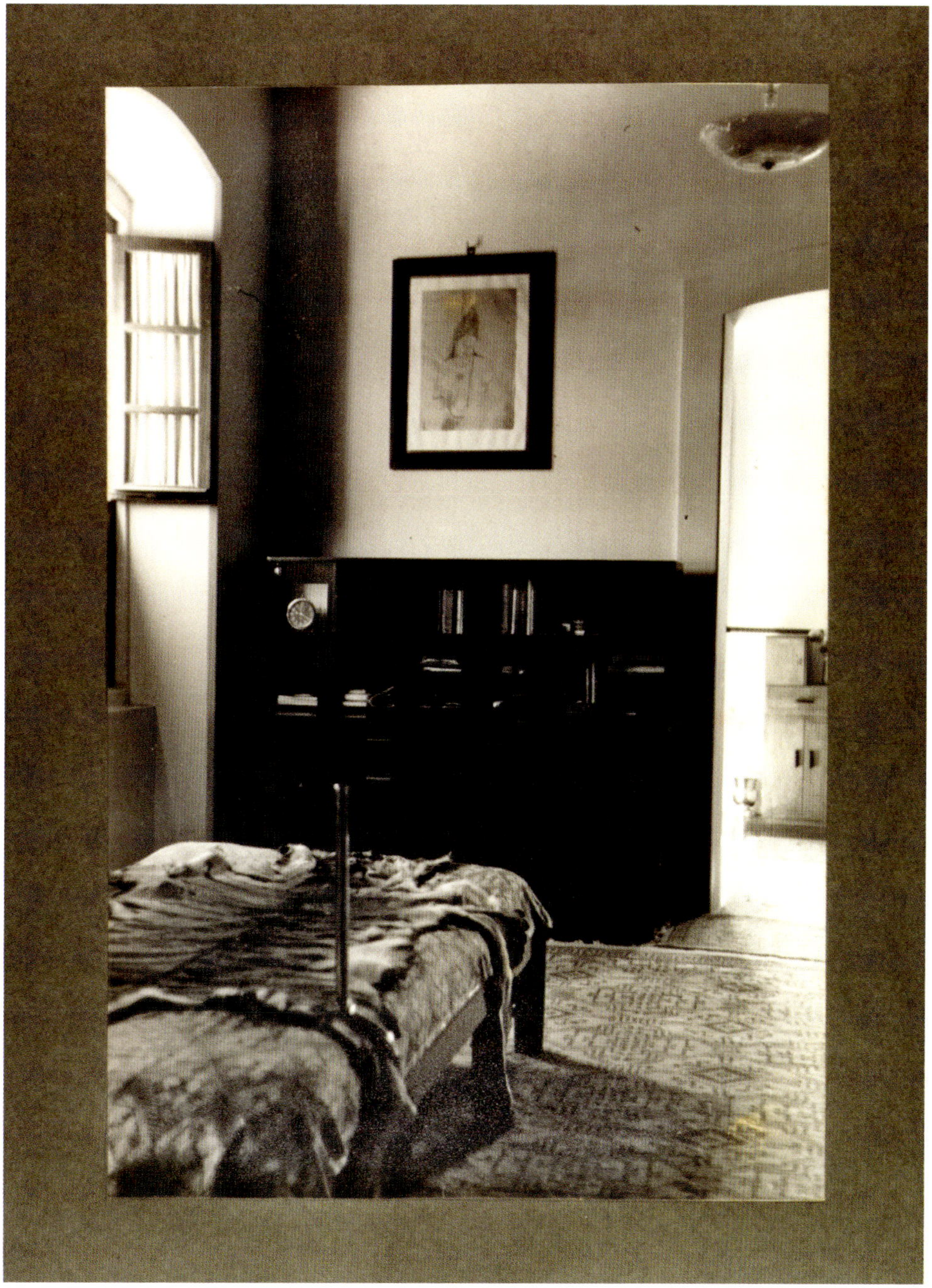

Fig. 24
Henri Cartier-Bresson
[Room of Sri Aurobindo Ghosh] from the album 'Sri Aurobindo and His Ashram,' April 1950, Gelatin Silver Print, 403 x 315 mm
ACP: D2005.06.0001(0119)

Note 762-17 from Bresson's personal diary
'Sri Aurobindo' s room and bed, with the inevitable tiger skin which seems the companion of those aiming at spiritual achievement.'

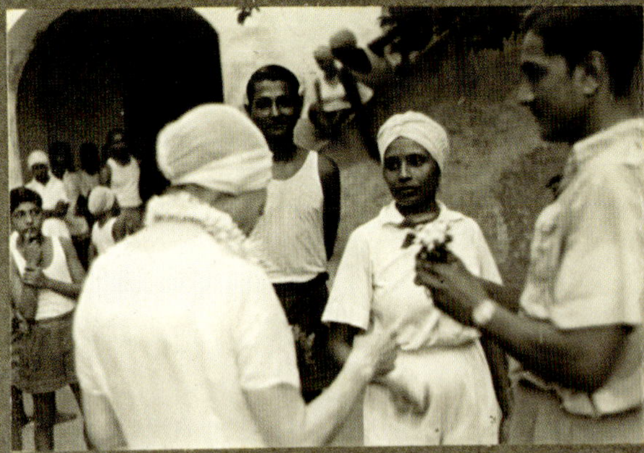

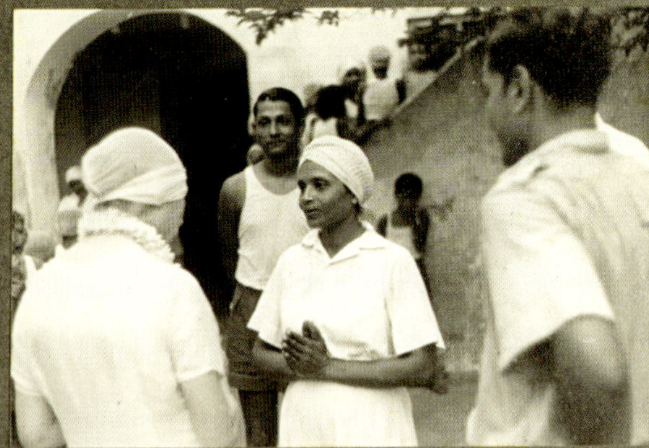

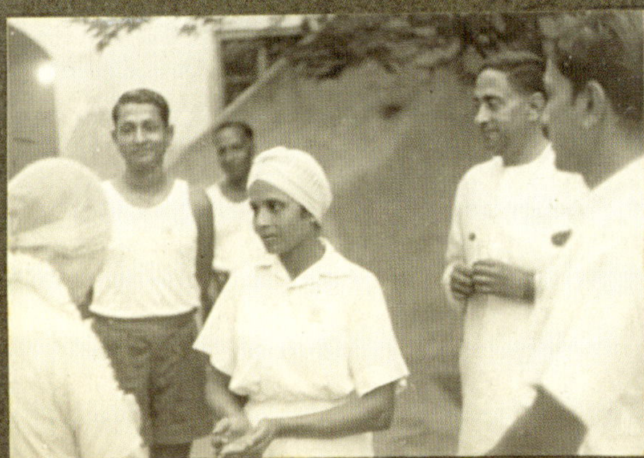

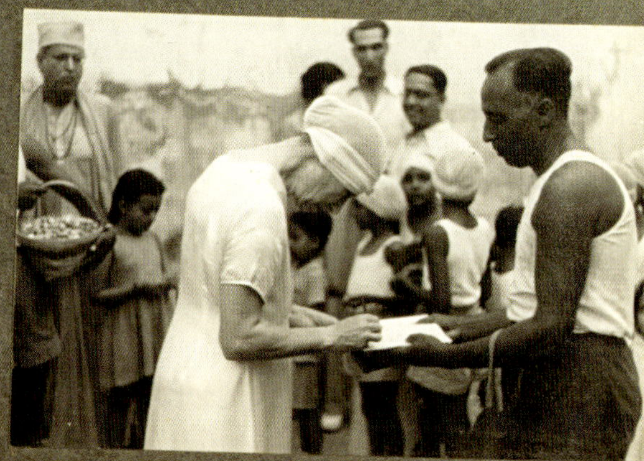

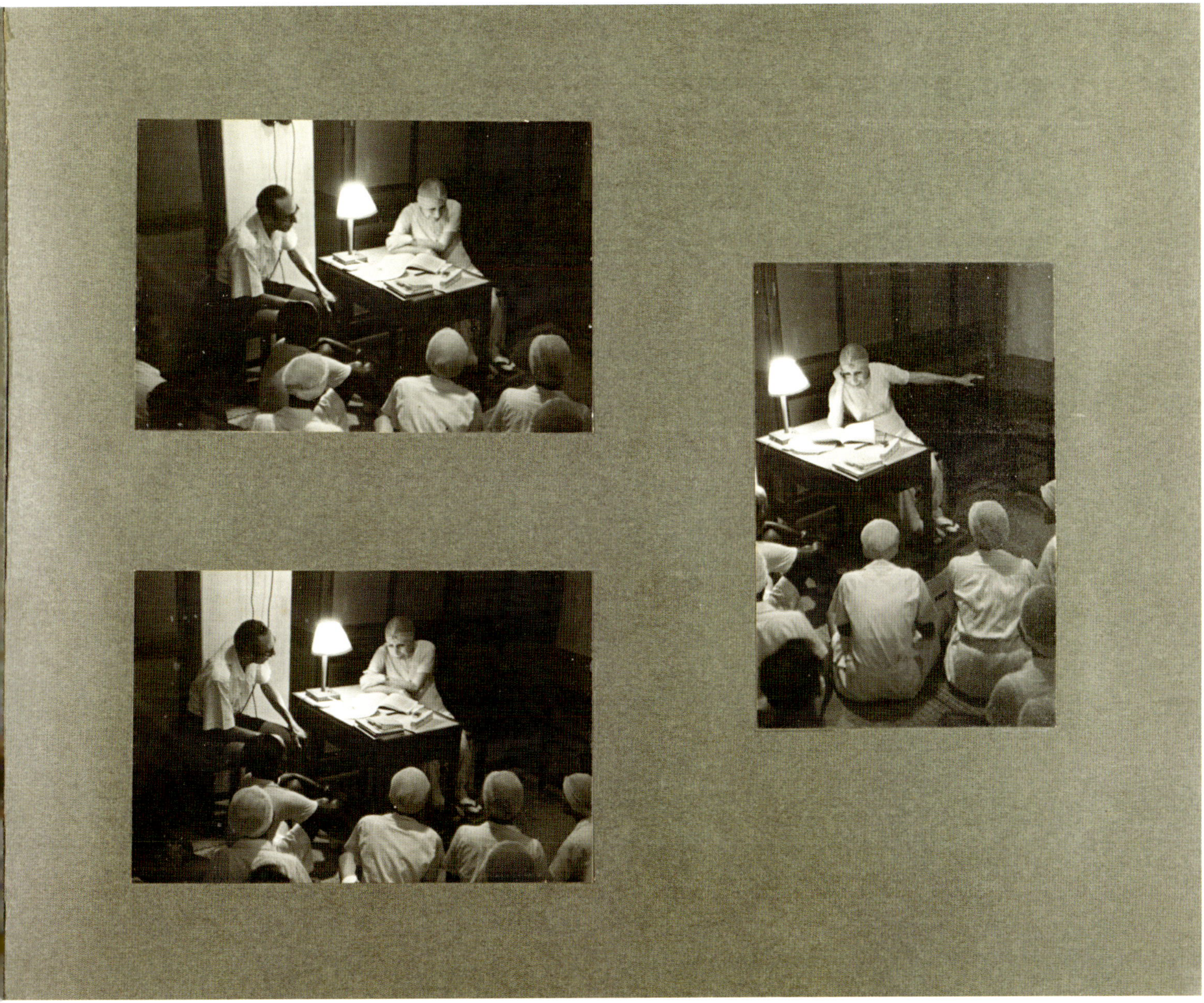

Fig. 23

Henri Cartier-Bresson

[Daily activities at the Ashram with the Mother] from the album 'Sri Aurobindo and His Ashram,' April 1950, Gelatin Silver Prints, 315 x 403 mm (each) ACP: D2005.06.0001(0103-110)

Personal Notes by Henri Cartier-Bresson as provided by the Henri Cartier-Bresson Foundation, Paris: 755.
Mother gives to every one according their needs; some outsiders hint that it is according to what they gave, but all this is a personal matter.

'ASHRAM PHOTOGRAPHY'

Photography was formally introduced to the Ashram by Chimanbhai Patel, a practitioner who had learnt photography in Nairobi, Kenya[41] and had come to Pondicherry in the late 1940s. He set up a photographic section known as The Photo Service in the Ashram, together with a darkroom and an enlarger in 1948.[42] With the passage of time, photography conducted by the photographers was officially termed 'Ashram Photography.' Two photographers present at the time, Pranab Kumar Bhattacharya[43] and Tara Jauhar helped to document the Mother as well as the activities of the Ashram, a collection that still remains in their archive. Additionally, Chimanbhai, Robi Ganguli[44] and Tara Jauhar helped Bresson develop some of his negatives and assisted in the actual making of the Sri Aurobindo Ashram Album.[45]

Most of the photographers had their own dark rooms with state-of-the-art cameras such as the Leica and Rolleiflex[46] for shooting and Omega, DeJure and Focomat enlargers for printing. During this period, Venkatesh, Vidyavrata, Robi and Kanak Ganguli participated regularly in national and international exhibitions in the 1950s and 60s such as The London Salon, The Royal Photographic Society (England), Bordeaux (France), FIAP (Switzerland), Swedish Master Competition (Sweden). Their works were also published in Photography Year Book, Photograms of the Year, and the FIAP Year Book. Some of the other active photographers were: Sanjiban Biswas, Biswajit Talukdar, Sudha Sundaram and Dr. Prabhat Sanyal.

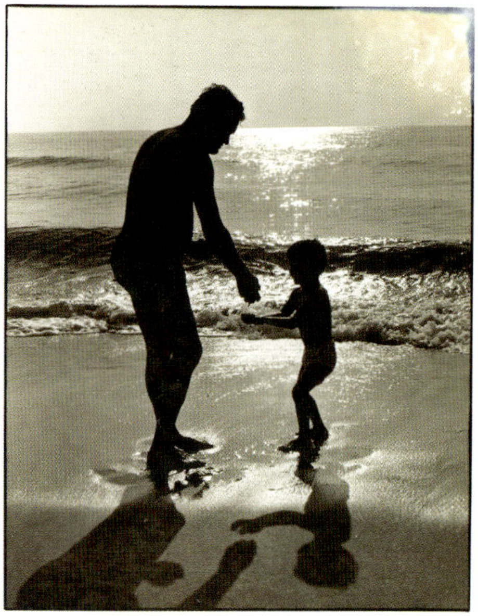

These photographers experimented with light, shapes and forms. The initial works of some artists-cum-photographers in the Ashram show a leaning towards the "pictorial"[47] paradigm [Fig. 25-34]. For instance, Venkatesh Shirodkar, a photographer residing in Pondicherry at the time was primarily a painter, which is evident in his selection of subjects, as well as the overall composition. On the other hand, Vidyavrata, was known for his technical agility, experimenting with his camera, especially with regard to portraiture and the use of trick photography [Fig 35–37]. In contrast, Tara Jauhar's works show a deep interest in visualising children, their dispositions and their moods [Fig. 38].

A remarkable phenomenon in the Ashram was a *Pondicherry International Photography Exhibition* spearheaded by Robi Ganguli, which received photographic entries internationally. Enthusiasts from more than 25 countries participated in the exhibition.[48] The first Pondicherry Salon of Photography opened to the public on 15 of August, 1955. It was conducted according to the recommended practices of the Photographic Society of America[49] and the International Federation of Photographic Art,[50] and was approved by both these bodies. However, it did not travel abroad nor were the photographs exhibited for commercial purposes. Unfortunately this annual exhibition (opening on the 15th of August every year) continued only till 1983. Sadly, it had to be discontinued due to problems with the Postal and Customs Department of Madras.

Above
Fig. 38
Tara Jauhar
Sri Aurobindo Ashram, Pondicherry
"Silver and Silhouette," c. 1948 – 1975,
Gelatin Silver Print, 362 x 289 mm
ACP: D2004.82.0041

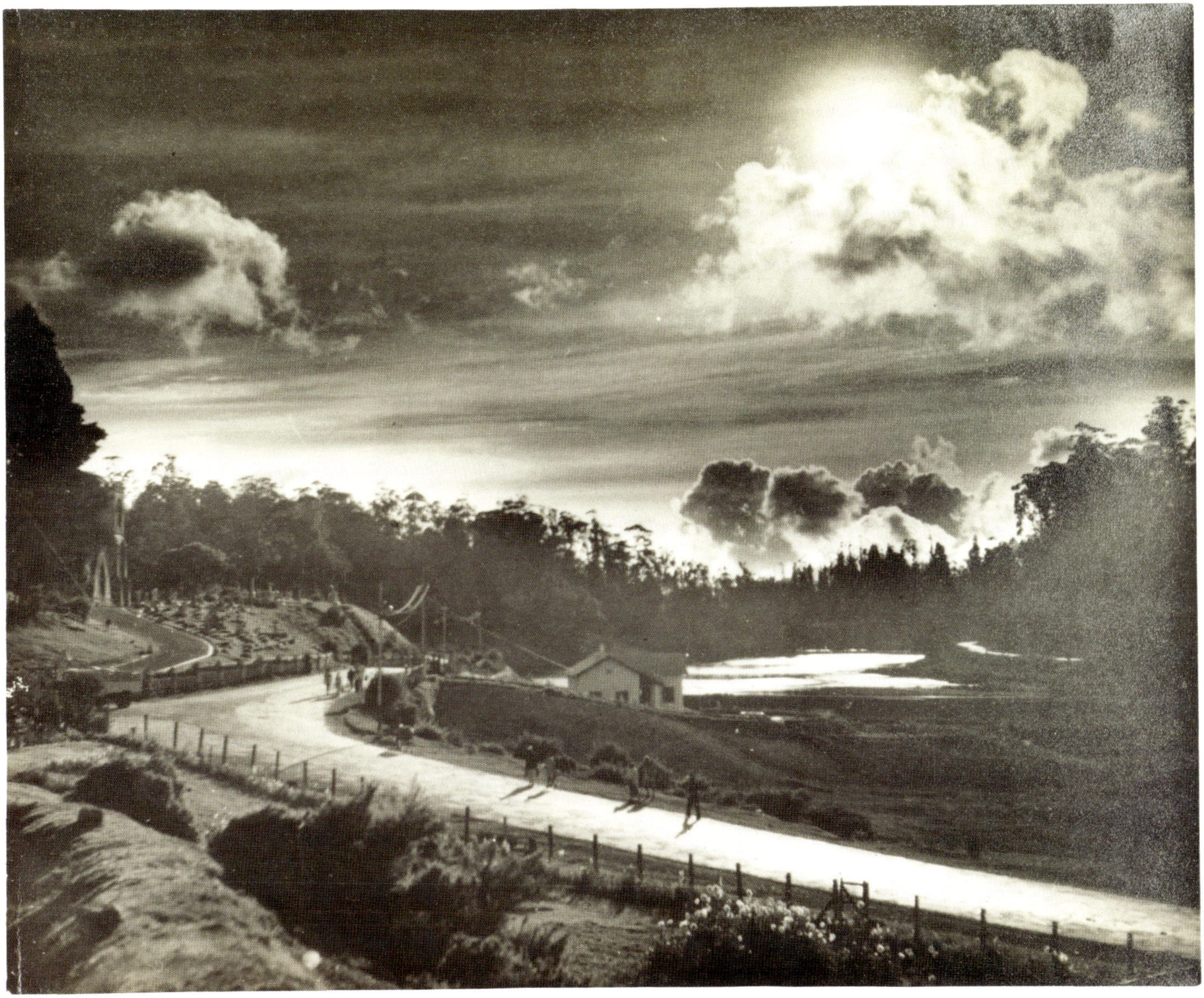

Fig. 25
Venkatesh Shirodkar
Sri Aurobindo Ashram, Pondicherry,
[Untitled Landscape], , c. 1948 - 1975
Gelatin Silver Print, 236 x 295 mm
ACP: D2004.82.0006

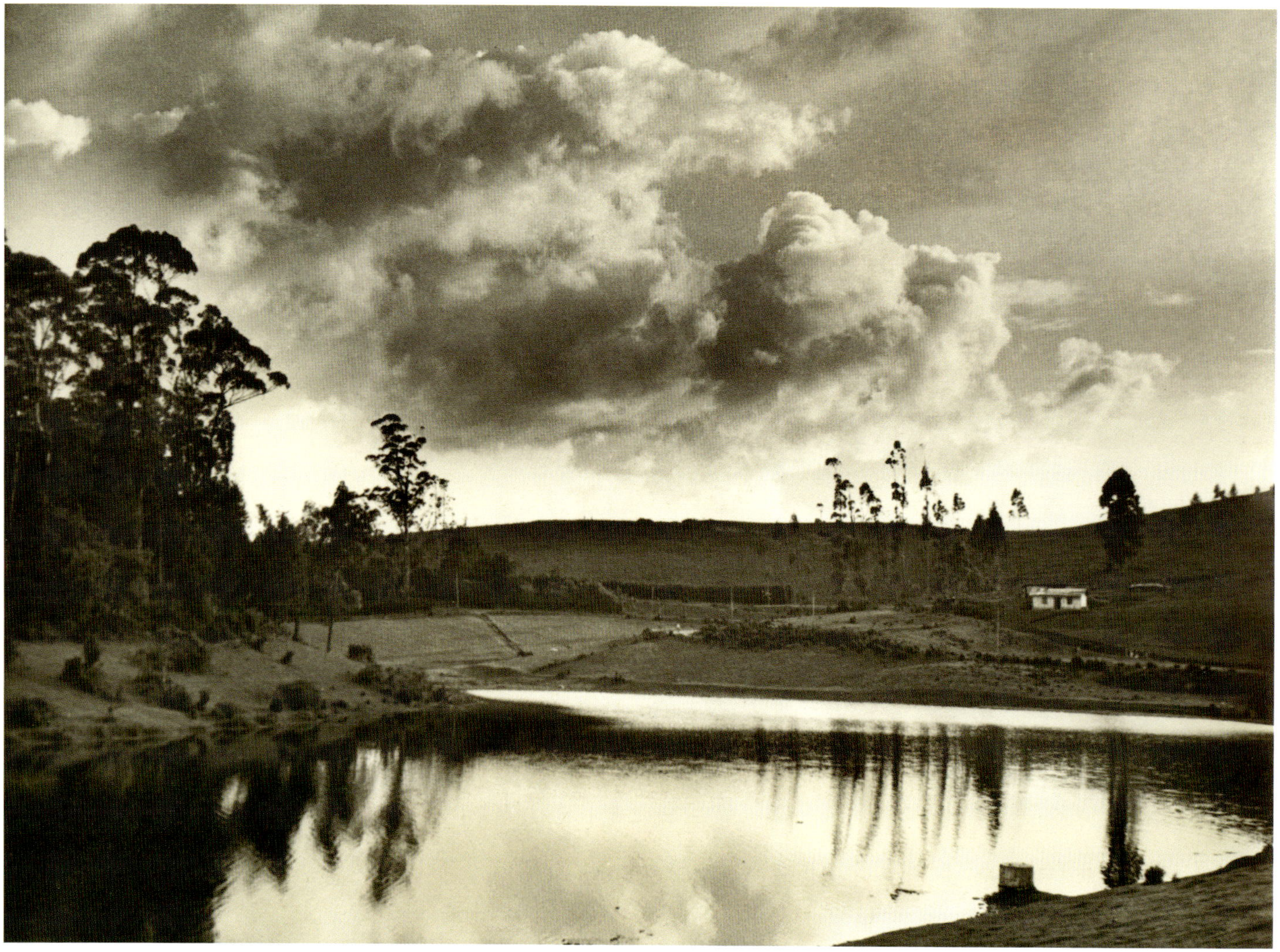

Fig. 26
Venkatesh Shirodkar
Sri Aurobindo Ashram, Pondicherry
[Untitled Landscape], c. 1948 - 1975
Gelatin Silver Print, 231 x 294 mm
ACP: D2004.82.0007

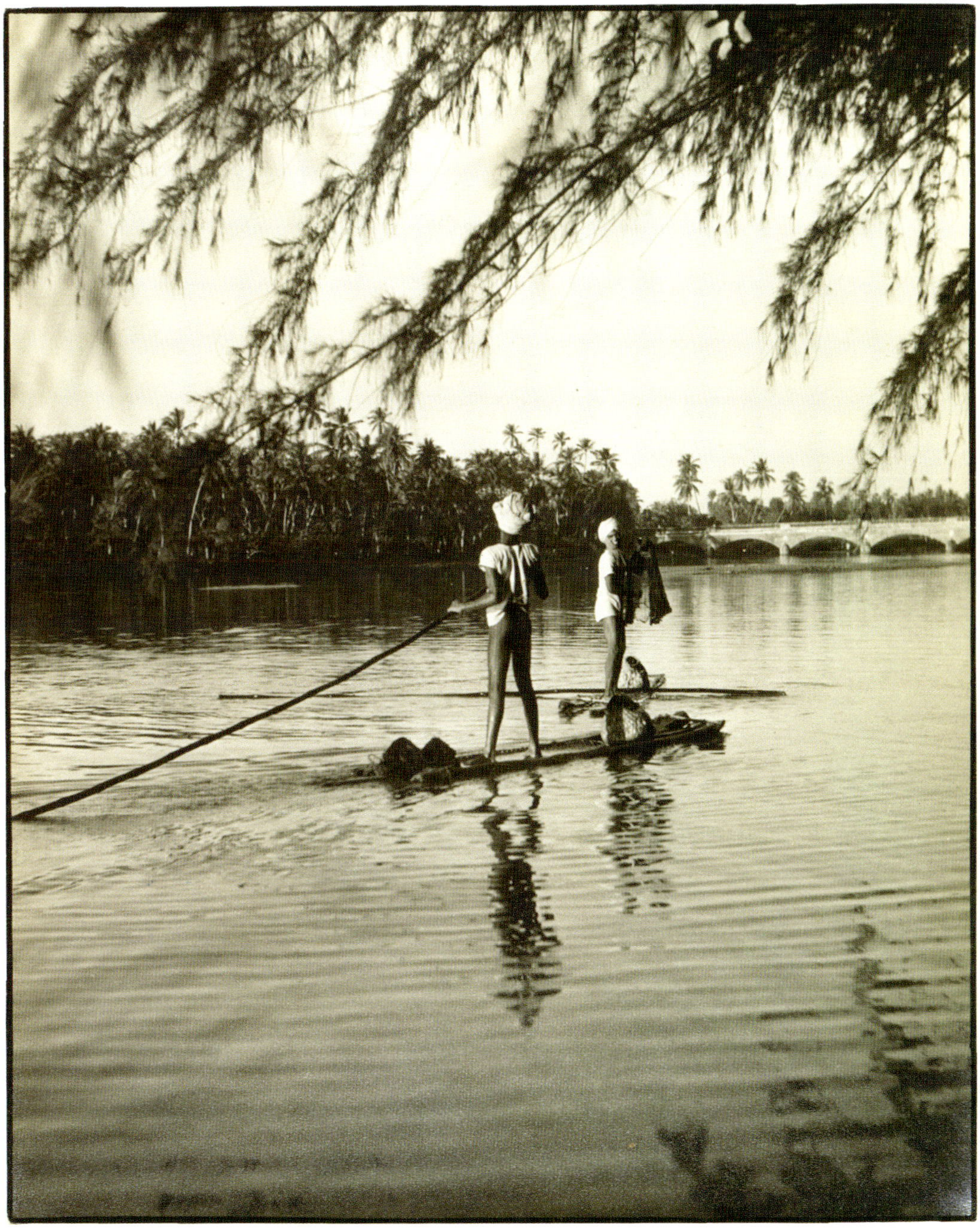

Fig. 27
Venkatesh Shirodkar
Sri Aurobindo Ashram, Pondicherry
"Snatch-Gossip," c. 1948 - 1975
Gelatin Silver Print, 289 x 237 mm
ACP: D2004.82.0021

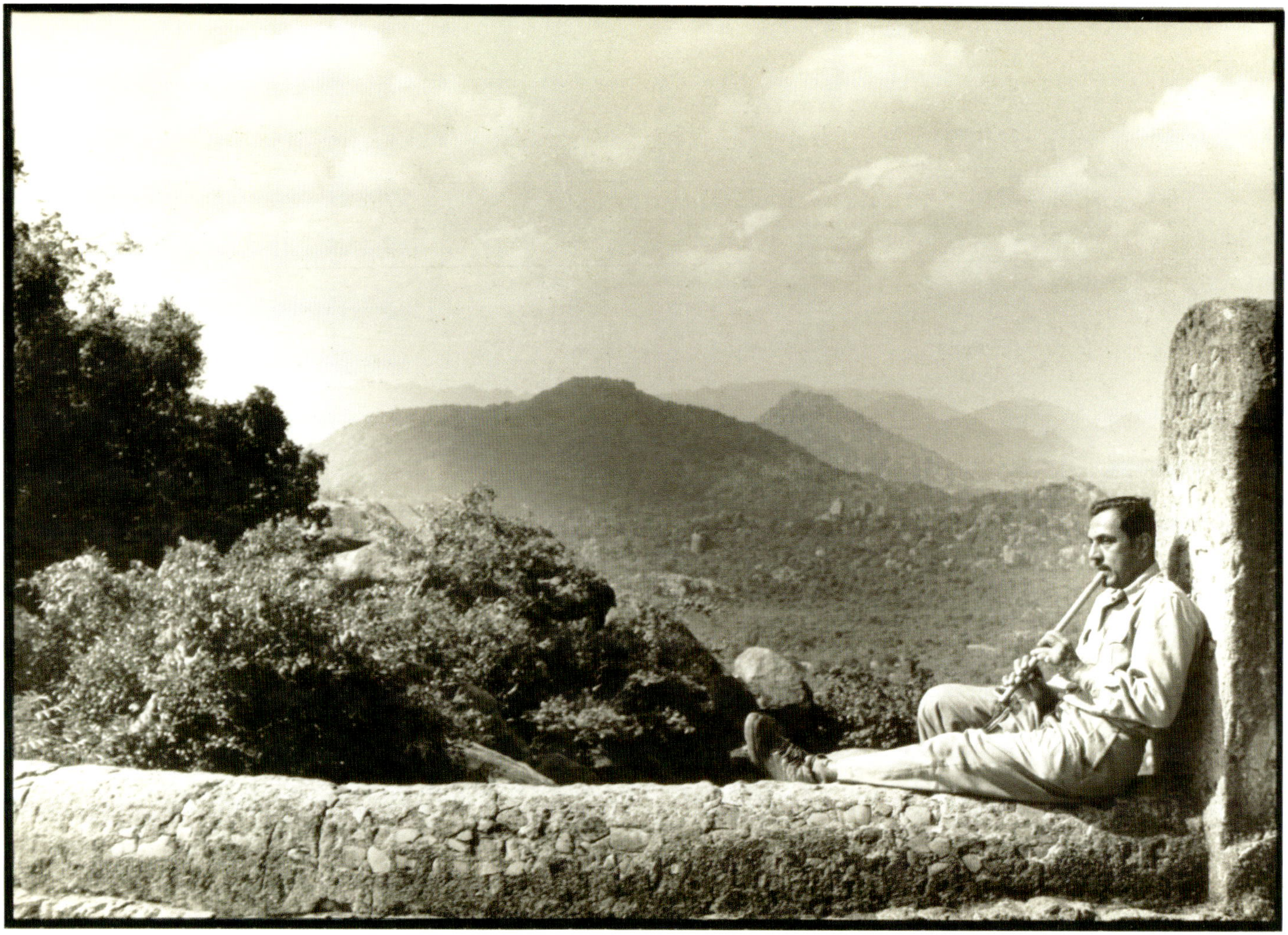

Fig. 28
Tara Jauhar
Sri Aurobindo Ashram, Pondicherry
"Modern Krishna In tune with nature" [The person in the picture is Pranab Kumar Bhattacharya], 1975, Gelatin Silver Print, 255 x 363 mm
ACP: D2004.82.0037

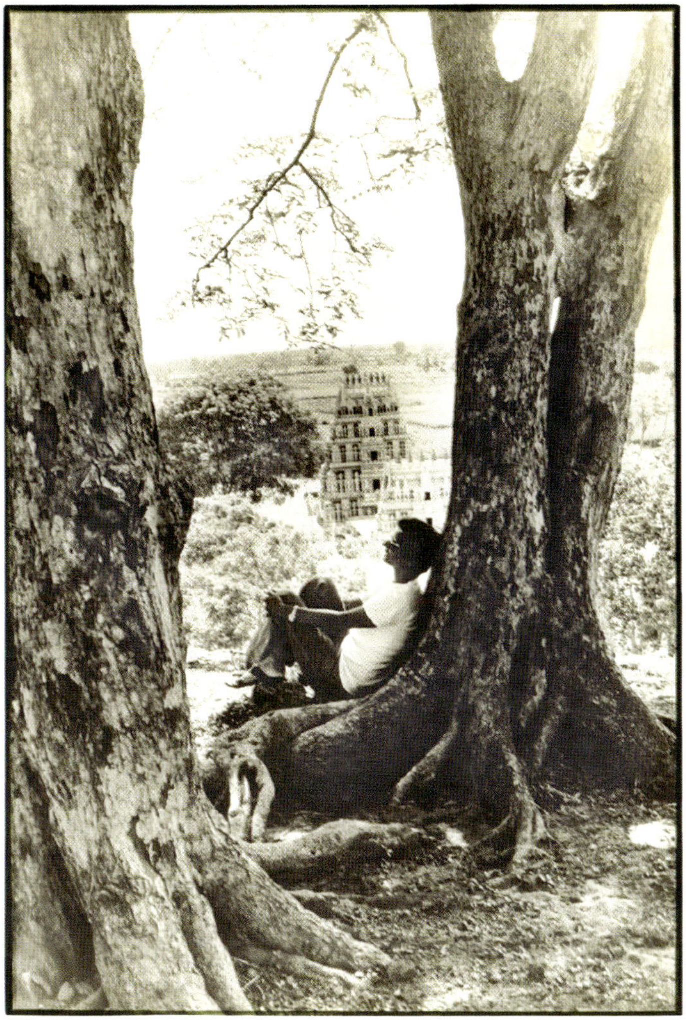

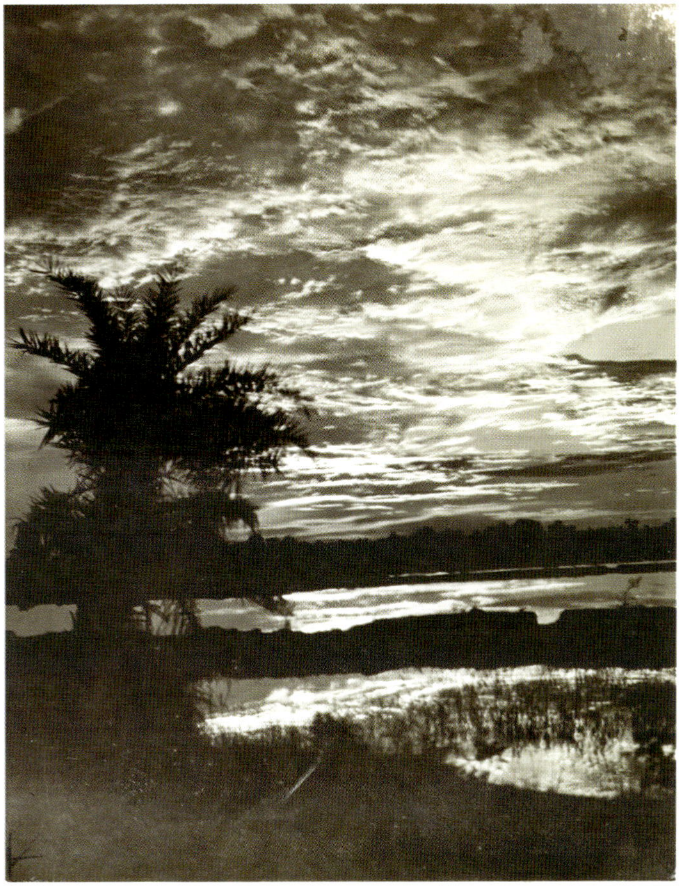

Fig. 29
Pranab Kumar Bhattacharya
Sri Aurobindo Ashram Saloon, Pondicherry
[Untitled Portrait]
[The person in the picture is Tara Jauhar.], 1975,
Gelatin Silver Print, 364 x 249 mm
ACP: D2004.82.0029

Fig. 30
Vidyavratta (Attribution)
[Untitled Landscape], c. 1948 - 1975
Gelatin Silver Print, 366 x 290 mm
ACP: D2004.82.0025

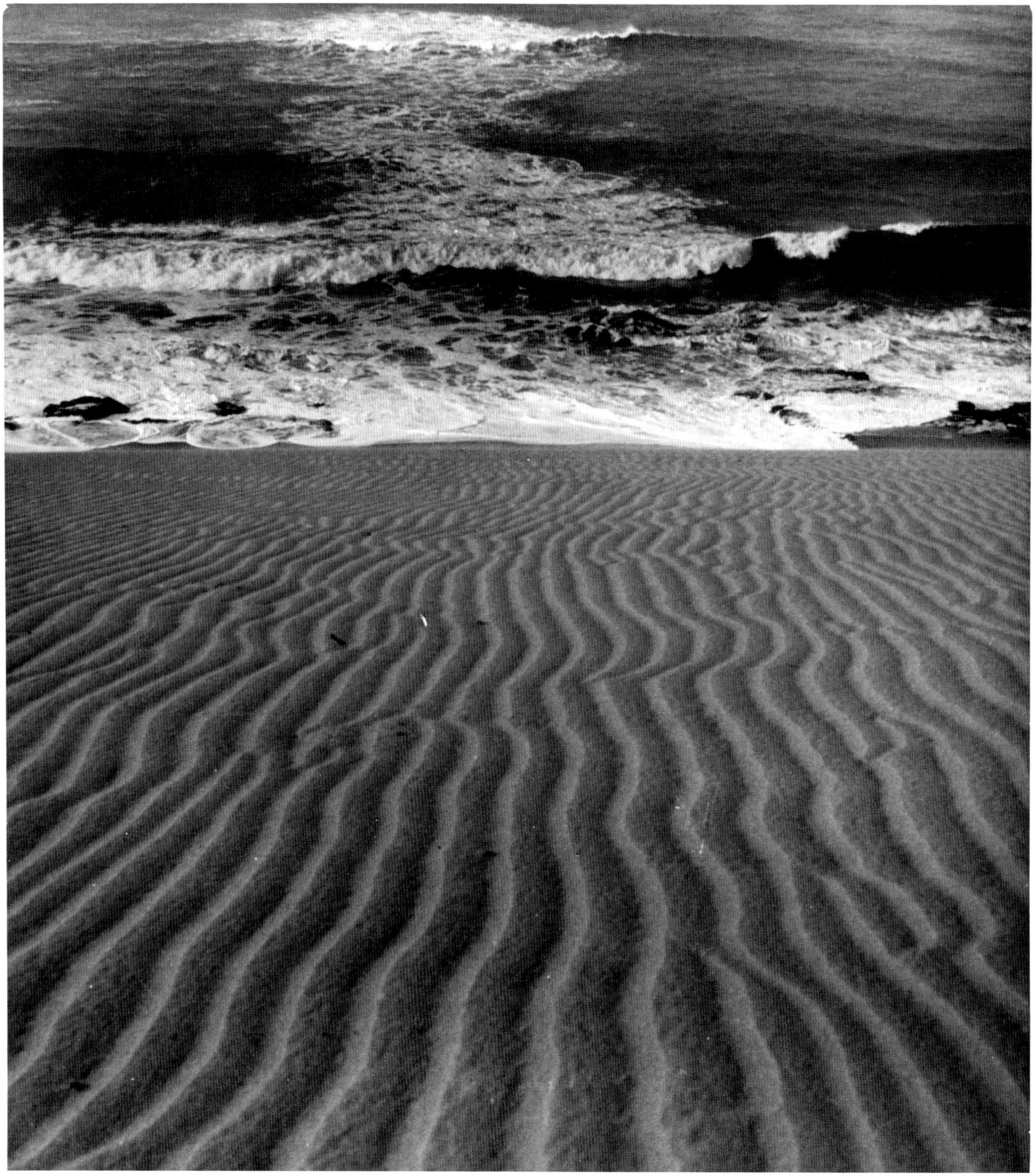

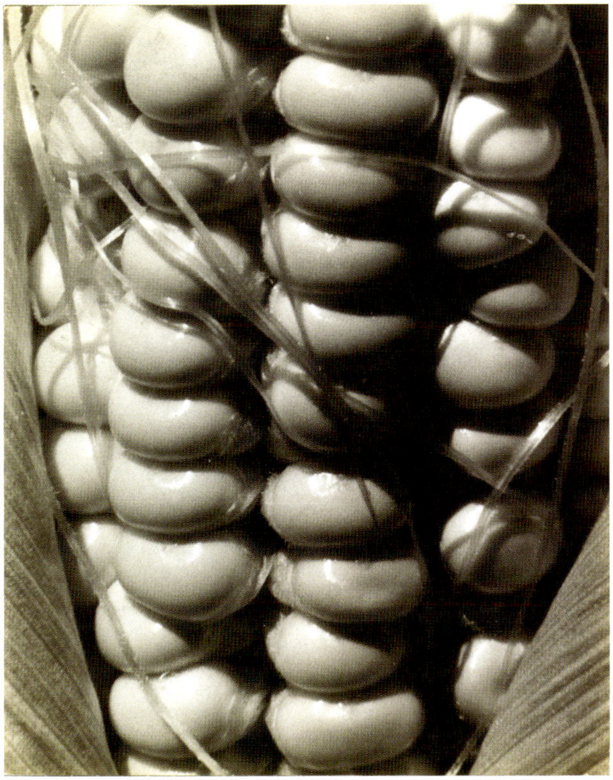

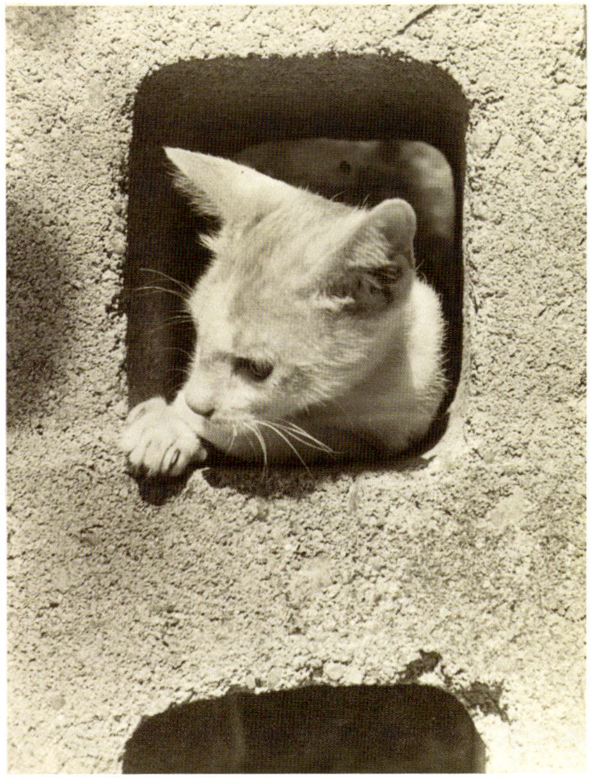

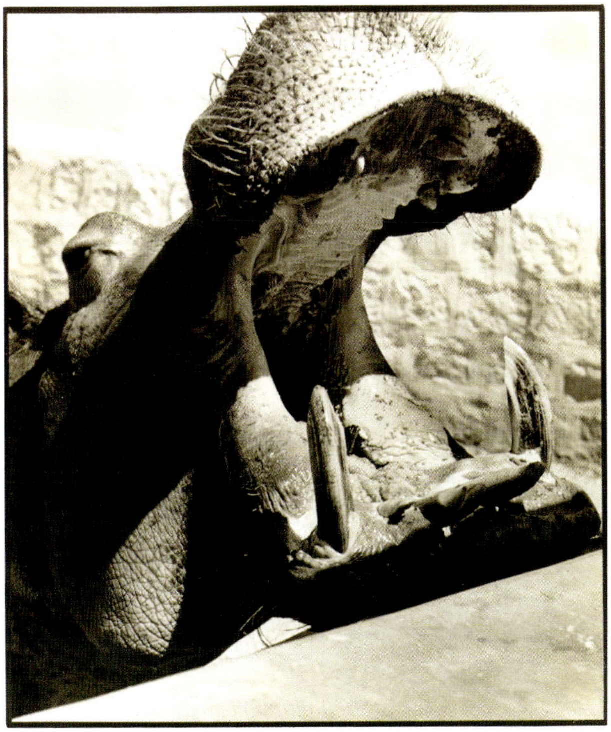

Left, above
Fig. 32
Venkatesh Shirodkar
Sri Aurobindo Ashram, Pondicherry
"Name it," c. 1948 - 1975
Gelatin Silver Print, 237 x 293 mm
ACP: D2004.82.0014

Above
Fig. 33
Venkatesh Shirodkar
Sri Aurobindo Ashram, Pondicherry
[Life study], c. 1948 - 1975
Gelatin Silver Print, 290 x 225 mm
ACP: D2004.82.0018

Left
Fig. 34
Tara Jauhar
Sri Aurobindo Ashram, Pondicherry
"The Dentist's Nightmare," c. 1960
Gelatin Silver Print, 339 x 290 mm
ACP: D2004.82.0031

Facing page
Fig. 31
Venkatesh Shirodkar
Sri Aurobindo Ashram, Pondicherry
[Untitled Landscape], c. 1948 - 1975
Gelatin Silver Print, 274 x 241 mm
ACP: D2004.82.0005

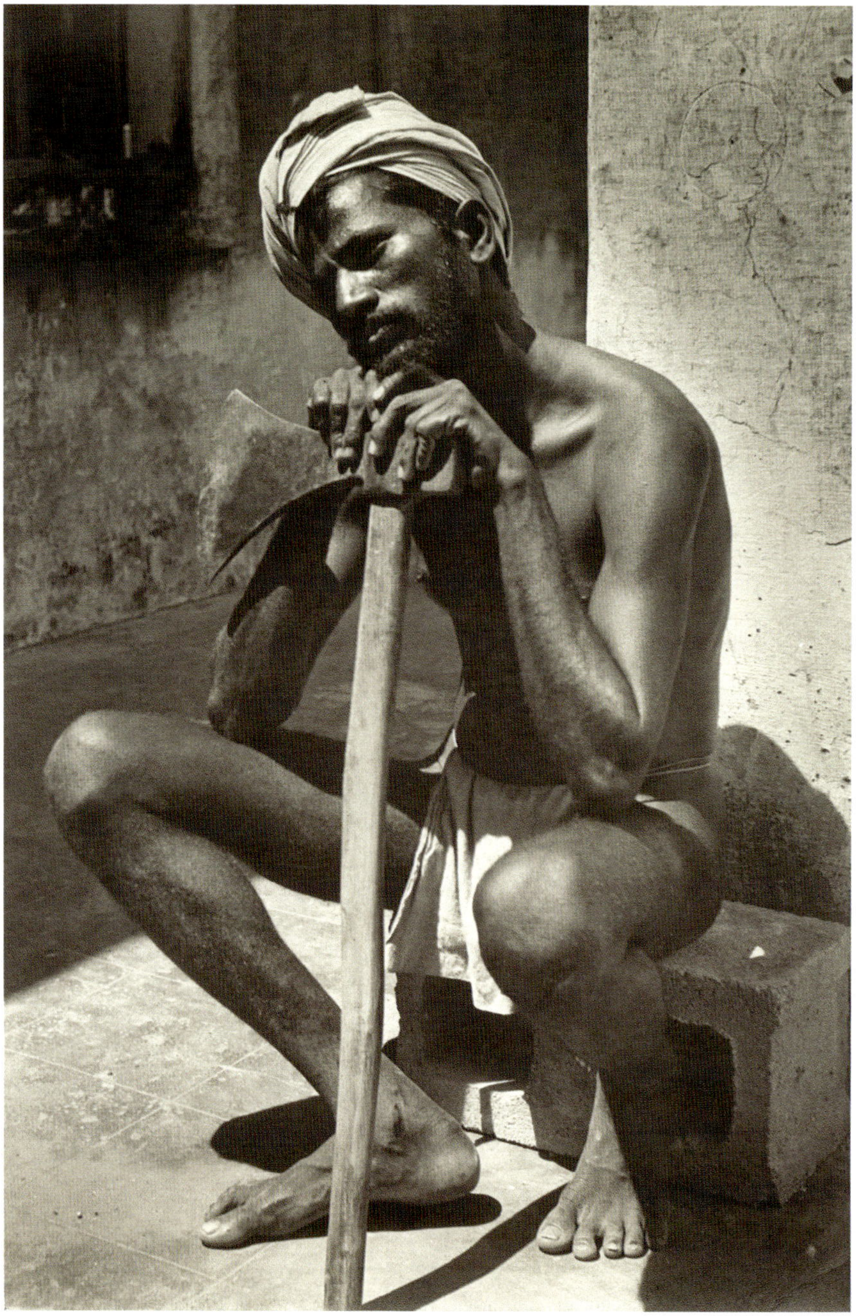

Fig. 35
Venkatesh Shirodkar
Shri Aurobindo Ashram, Pondicherry
[Untitled Portrait], c. 1948 - 1975
Gelatin Silver Print, 293 x 202 mm
ACP: D2004.82.0004

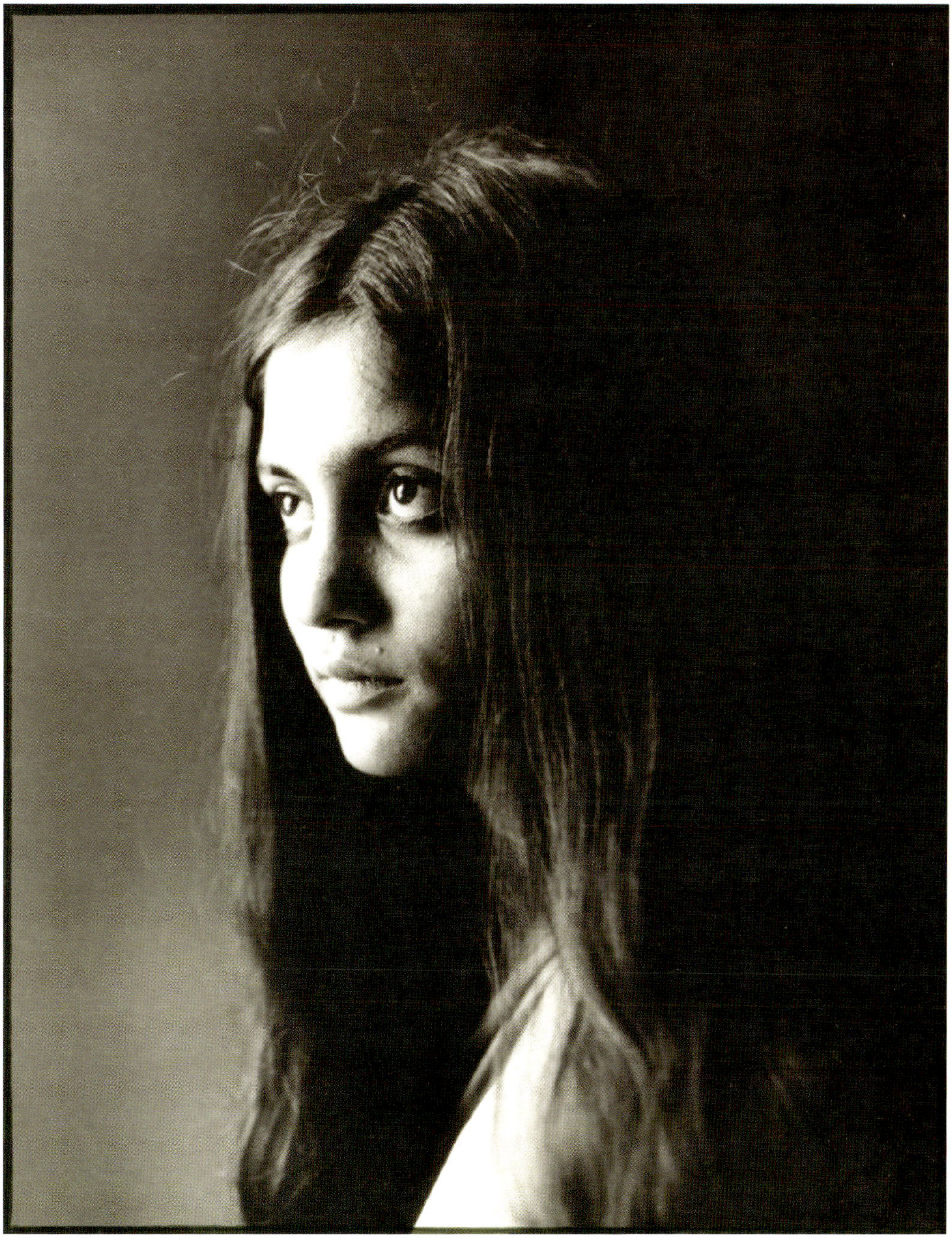

Fig. 36
Vidyavratta (Attribution)
Sri Aurobindo Ashram, Pondicherry
[Untitled Portrait], c. 1948 - 1975
Gelatin Silver Print, 366 x 290 mm
ACP: D2004.82.0025

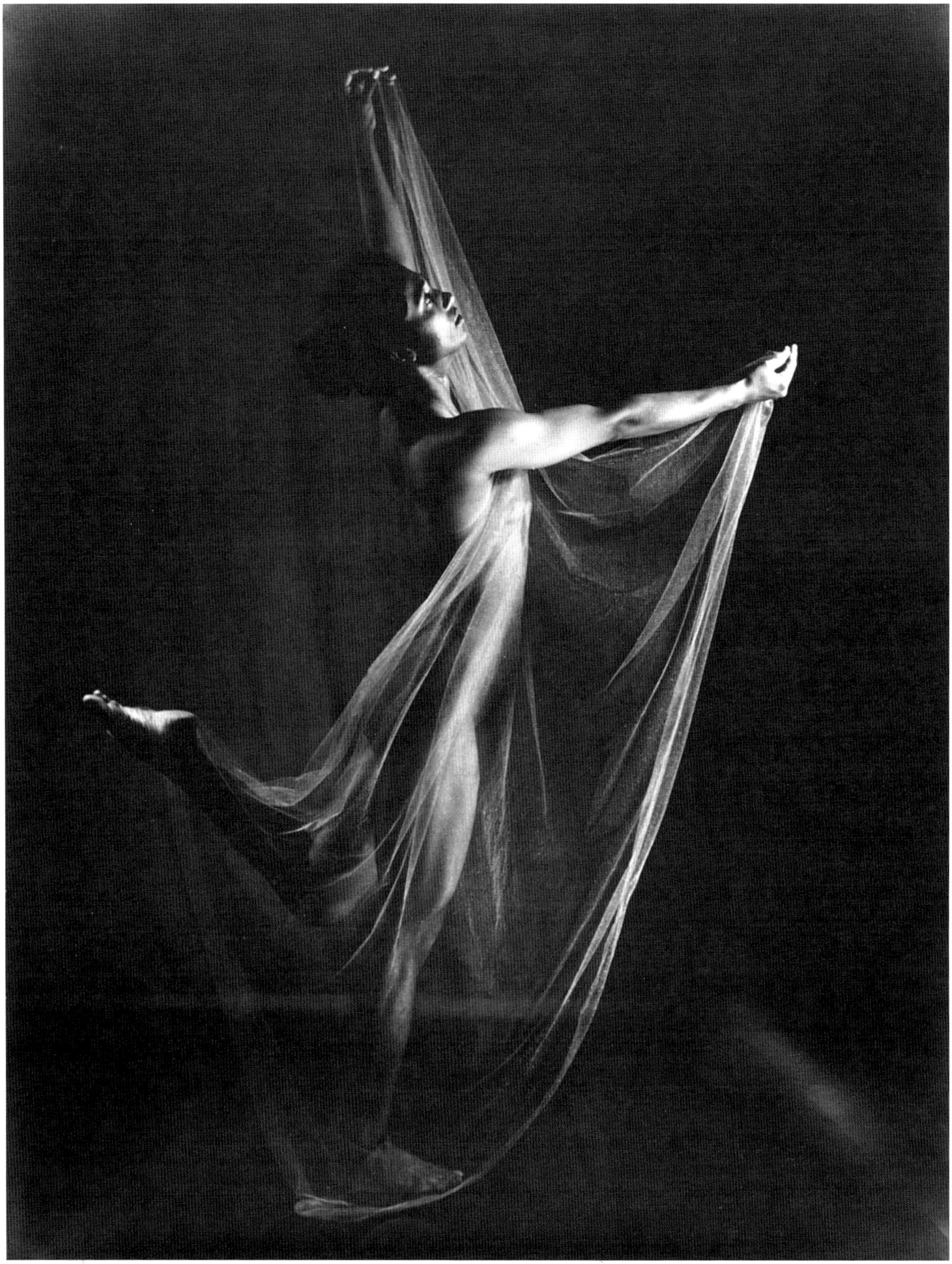

IN CONCLUSION

Memory is very important, the memory of each photo taken, flowing at the same speed as the event.

Henri Cartier-Bresson

Photographs are visual objects engaged with social space and real time,[51] and hence, there can be no single history of photography.[52] A photograph is a particular sort of image, one that operates through freezing a moment in time, portraying objects, people and places as they appear in front of the camera at that moment. Photography can also undermine the linear structure of a conventional narrative through an awareness that the visual is constitutive of the social and political realities we live in and not merely illustrative or reflective of them.[53] Thereby it contributes to the dislocation of time and space, enlightening and enlivening history and geography. If this be true, and if 'history' is the gathering together of documents, artifacts and related materials that narrate the past, what role does photography have in that process? Conversely, what role do histories play in an account of photography?[54]

Through the article, there has been an attempt to deconstruct the production of an album as a significant marker of personal and cultural history- not only by virtue of the photographer involved but also the consumer of it. Interestingly, after Bresson shot the Ashram, a collection of images was published by him as part of Magnum photos in *Illustrated*.[55] Subsequently, the Sri Aurobindo Ashram received popular criticism about the spiritual leader of the Ashram, Sri Aurobindo as a 'living god' among other beings. Upon receiving such information, the Mother insisted on purchasing all the photographs and negatives from Magnum Photos, details of which are mentioned earlier in the article.

The current compilation is therefore not by Bresson, but by the Mother, who purchased the copyright and made a photo-testimony, dedicated to the Ashram; a collaborative exercise done in isolation of the photographer. Consequently, apart from being shot by Bresson, the album preserves and commemorates events, activities, accomplishments with an interplay of memory, and chronology[56] within the Ashram as a microcosm. The authorial nature of this album, as is the case with several others from the 19th century, represents the mindset of the album-maker in conjunction with the temperament of the photographer. On the other hand, the local history of photography in the Ashram offers an array of ideas signaling its development as a space to which practitioners were drawn but also one that harboured photography as an art practice. It is with testimony to these facts that the array of material featured here suggests the presence of a strong local tradition which was influenced and developed by a larger global one.

To end, quoting Alan Sekula in his article "Reading the Archive", 'in an archive, the possibility of meaning is "liberated" from the actual contingencies of use. This liberation is also a loss, an abstraction from the complexity and richness of use, a loss of context'. Archives, therefore, play an important function in the creation of knowledge, moving back in time rather than looking at history as a starting point alone.[57] Characteristically, an archive seeks to grow; it aspires to completeness and through this process of mass acquisition a distinct kind of knowledge emerges.[58] The main objective of this essay is therefore not linear—to bring out a biography of photography in Pondicherry, but to tap into the simultaneity of its many parallel histories through the existence of available visual material.

Facing page
Fig. 37
Tara Jauhar
Sri Aurobindo Ashram, Pondicherry
"Truth Transparent," c. 1948 - 1975
Gelatin Silver Print, 371 x 289 mm
ACP: D2004.82.0026

ENDNOTES

1 Ramaswamy, Sumathi (Ed.). *Beyond Appearances: Visual Practices and Ideologies in Modern India*. New Delhi: Sage, 2003, p. xvi.

2 Falconer, John and Satish Sharma. *A Shifting Focus: Photography in India 1850-1900*. The British Council and British Library, 1995, p. 9-10.

3 Mitter, Partha, Akshaya Tankha, Suryanandini Sinha and Rahaab Allana. *The Artful Pose: Early Studio Photography in Mumbai c. 1855 – 1940*. New Delhi: The Alkazi Collection of Photography and Mapin Publishing, 2010, p. 9.

4 Pinney, Christopher. *Camera Indica: The Social Life of Indian Photographs*. London: Reaktion Books, 1997, p. 17.

5 Allana, Rahaab and Pramod Kumar K.G. *Painted Photographs: Coloured Portraiture in India*. New Delhi: The Alkazi Collection of Photography and Mapin Publishing, 2008.

6 Wells, Liz. *Photography: A Critical Introduction*. Oxon: Routledge, 2009, p. 56.

7 The Coromandel Coast is the name given by the Europeans to the southeastern coast of the Indian Subcontinent between Cape Comorin (Kanyakumari) and False Divi Point (in Andhra Pradesh). The coast is known for its ports and harbours such as Pulicat, Chennai (Madras), Sadras, Pondicherry, Karaikal, Cuddalore, Tranquebar, Nagore, and Nagapattinam.

8 Lafont, Jean-Marie. *Chitra Cities and Monuments of Eighteenth-century India from French Archives*. New Delhi: Oxford University Press, 2001, p. 76

9 Ibid.

10 Joseph-François, Marquis Dupleix (1 January 1697 – 10 November 1763) was appointed as the Governor General of the French establishment in India in 1742. He succeeded Dumas as the French governor of Pondicherry. His ambition was to acquire for France vast territories in India, and for this purpose he entered into relations with the native princes, and adopted a style of oriental splendour in his dress and surroundings. He built an army of native troops, called sepoys, who were trained as infantrymen men in his service also included the famous Hyder Ali of Mysore. During his posting, many French architectural masterpieces were built all across Pondicherry in the French Settlements there.

11 [By an Officer of the Madras Artillery], *Notes on Pondicherry; or The French in India*. Calcutta: W.Thacker and Co., 1845, p. 10-11.

12 Sen, S.P. *The French in India: 1763-1816*. Calcutta: Firma K.L. Mukhopadhyay, 1958, p. 57

13 *Architectural Heritage of Pondicherry: Tamil and French Precincts*. Pondicherry: INTACH Pondicherry Chapter, 2001, p. 58.

14 Ibid., p. 13.

15 Nilsson, Sten. *European Architecture in India 1750-1850*. London: Faber and Faber, 1968, p. 95.

16 Ibid.

17 Sen, S.P. *The French in India: 1763-1816*. Calcutta: Firma K.L. Mukhopadhyay, 1958, p. 57.

18 Institut Francais de Pondichery 2007. http://www.ifpindia.org/ecrire/upload/digital_database/Site/Pondi/data/part_2_1_2_pier.html.

19 Bourne & Shepherd established in 1863 by Samuel Bourne and Charles Shepherd, is the oldest photographic studio still in operation, and one of the oldest established photographic businesses in the world. At its peak it was the most successful commercial firm in 19th-and early 20th-century India, with agencies all over India, and outlets in London and Paris. They also ran a mail order service. [Drawn from: Osbourne, Peter D., *Travelling Light: Photography, Travel and Visual Culture*. Manchester: Manchester University Press, 2000, p. 44-46.]

20 Falconer, John and Satish Sharma. *A Shifting Focus: Photography in India 1850-1900*. The British Council and British Library, 1995, p. 18.

21 Ibid, p. 19.

22 Falconer, John. *India: Pioneering Photographers 1850 – 1900*. London: The British Library and The Howard and Jane Ricketts Collection, 2001.

23 Wells, Liz. *Photography: A Critical Introduction*. Oxon: Routledge, 2009, p. 305.

24 This is achieved by positioning the focal plane of the camera at so that it is perpendicular to the ground, regardless of the elevation of the camera eye.

25 Michell, George (Ed.). *Vijayanagara: Splendour in Ruins*. New Delhi: The Alkazi Collection of Photography and Mapin Publishing, 2008, p. 166-167.

26 Curtis, Verna Posever (Ed.). *Photographic Memory: The Album in the Age of Photography*. New York: Aperture, Library of Congress, 2011, p. 7.

27 Ibid.

28 http://www.sriaurobindoashram.org/ashram/sriauro/index.php

29 Ibid.

30 http://www.sriaurobindoashram.org/ashram/mother/index.php

31 "Darshan" in Sanskrit means "seeing". It refers here to seeing Sri Aurobindo and the Mother and to receive their blessings. After Sri Aurobindo retired from daily contact with his disciples, he saw them only a few times a year on what came to be known as the Darshan days. Sri Aurobindo interrupted his retirement four times a year when he appeared before his disciples. This was always a great day at Pondicherry for which devotees from all parts of Bengal, Gujarat and elsewhere (including foreigners) arrived. Flower sellers posted themselves at the entrance of the Ashram and the devotees bought garlands for Sri Aurobindo and the Mother.

32 Magnum Photos Inc. Story #59, Photogrpaher: Henri Cartier-Bresson. [Courtesy: HCB Foundation]

33 Ibid.

34 http://www.sriaurobindoashram.org/research/show.php?set=doclife&id=31.

35 Ibid.

36 Ibid.

37 Magnum Photos Inc. Story #59, Photogrpaher: Henri Cartier-Bresson. [Courtesy: HCB Foundation]

38 Magnum Photos Inc. Story #59, Photogrpaher: Henri Cartier-Bresson. [Courtesy: HCB Foundation]

39 As narrated by Tara Jauhar on 12 July 2012 in a personal interview with Shilpi Goswami. Tara now heads Sri Aurobindo Ashram, Delhi.

40 http://www.sriaurobindoashram.org/research/show.php?set=doclife&id=31

41 As narrated by Tara Jauhar and Prof Kittu Reddy on 17 July 2012 in a telephonic interview with Shilpi Goswami. Prof. Reddy stays in Sri Aurobindo Ashram, Pondicherry.

42 As narrated by Tara Jauhar.

43 Pranab Kuman Bhattacharya headed the Department of Physical Education in the Ashram and also eventually headed the Photo Service in the Ashram.

44 Robi Ganguli is one of the first students of Chimanbhai alongwith Tara Jauhar and others. He is 80 years of age and currently lives in Pondicherry.

45 As narrated by Tara Jauhar.

46 A range of Cameras such as Leica, Rolliflex, Graflex, Minolta, Pentax, Super Ikonta etc. were being used.

47 Pictorialism is the name given to an international style and aesthetic movement that dominated photography during the later 19th and early 20th centuries. There is no standard definition of the term, but in general it refers to a style in which the photographer has somehow manipulated what would otherwise be a straightforward photograph as a means of "creating" an image rather than simply recording it. Typically, a pictorial photograph appears to lack a sharp focus (some more so than others), is printed in one or more colors other than black-and-white (ranging from warm brown to deep blue) and may have visible brush strokes or other manipulation of the surface. For the pictorialist, a photograph, like a painting, drawing or engraving, was a way of projecting an emotional intent into the viewer's realm of imagination. [Drawn from: Bate, David. *Photography: The Key Concepts*. Oxford: Berg, 2009, p. 137 – 140]

48 For further reading refer to Prof. Kittu Reddy's article in this publication.

49 The Photographic Society of America (PSA) is a worldwide organization for anyone interested in photography. The society includes casual shutterbugs, serious amateurs, and professional photographers. Founded in 1934, PSA has members in over 70 countries. Individual, Club, and Council memberships offer a wide variety of services and activities: a monthly magazine; online photo galleries, image evaluation, study groups, and courses; competitions; an annual conference; recognition; and discounts on photography related products and services.

50 La FIAP was founded by DR. M. Van de Wijer, a Belgian, who has established links between different national photographic associations through the world, since 1946. Its purpose is the promotion of photographic art under all its aspects and by all kinds of photographic events. All considerations of political, ideological or racial order are absolutely banned from the activities of FIAP. The first Congress, the official act of the fondation of FIAP, took place in Bern (Switzerland) in 1950, with the participation of delegates from 10 countries. The FIAP is an international federation which affiliates as operational members, the national associations of photography. FIAP counts more than 85 national associations in the five continents and represents the benefits of nearly one million individual photographers.

51 Edwards, Elizabeth. *Raw Histories: Photographs, Anthropology and Museums*. Oxford: Berg, 2001, p. 2.

52 Wells, Liz (Ed.). *The Photography Reader*. Oxon: Routledge, 2003, p. 2

53 Ramaswamy, Sumathi (Ed.). *Beyond Appearances: Visual Practices and Ideologies in Modern India*. New Delhi: Sage, 2003, p. 2.

54 Bate, David. *Photography: The Key Concepts*. Oxford: Berg, 2009, p. 9.

55 http://www.sriaurobindoashram.org/research/show.php?set=doclife&id=31

Extract from letter Saint-Hilaire to Cartier-Bresson, 13 January 1950. Translated from the French.
"... We have received the issues of Heute and of Illustrated that published some of your photographs. Regarding Heute there is little to say: not brilliant, but passable. But as for Illustrated it is distressing to say the least. The photographs, like all of yours, are fine; but the selection, the arrangement and particularly the captions show a clear defamatory bias. The accompanying article is unspeakably vulgar and shows a complete lack of understanding."

56 Ibid.

57 Sekula, Alan. 'Reading an Archive' in Brian Wallis and Marcia Tucker (eds) Blasted Allegories, Cambridge, MA: MIT Press, 1991, p. 36

58 Wells, Liz (Ed.). *Photography: A Critical Introduction*, London: Routledge, 1997, p. 63-64, 339.

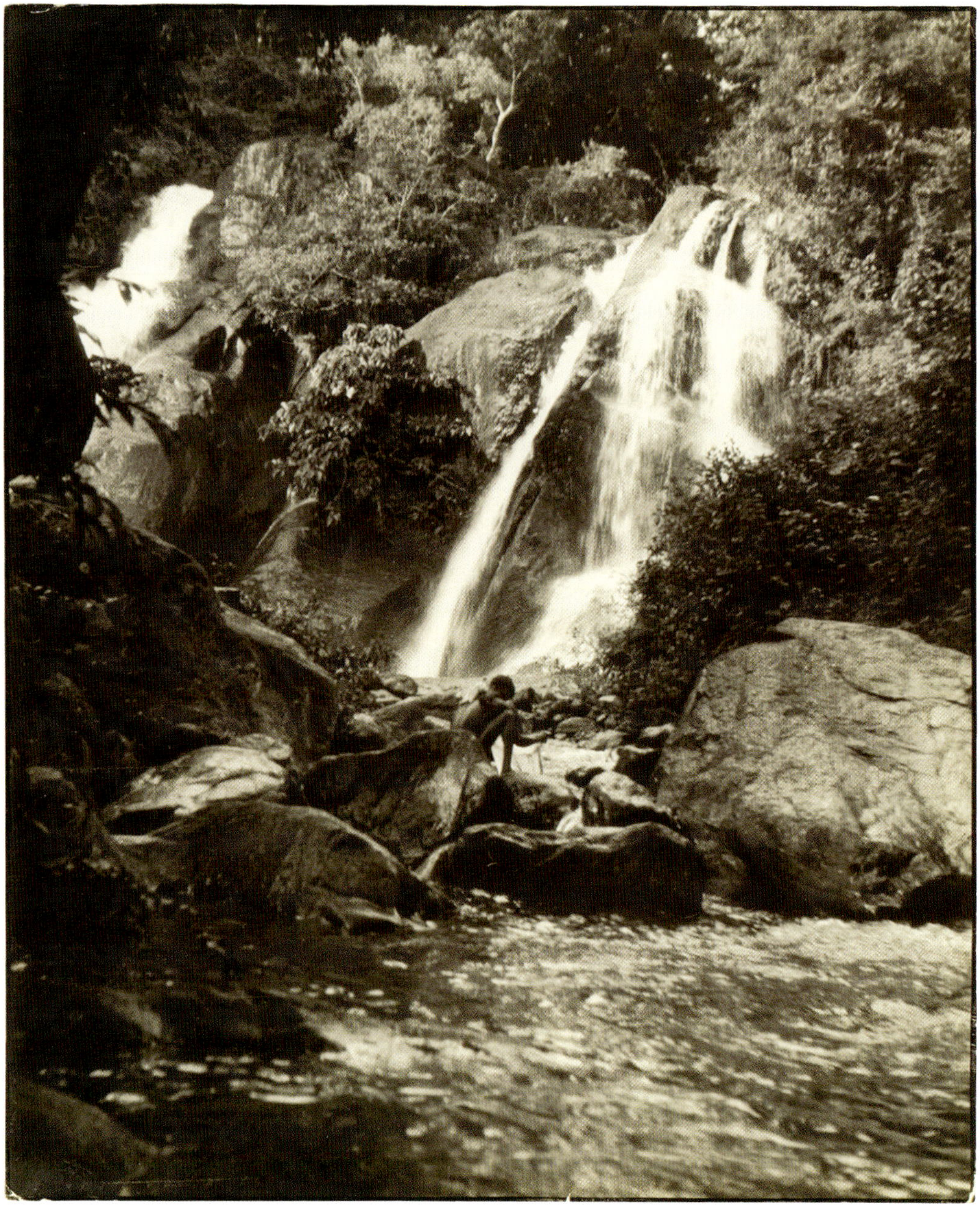

Venkatesh Shirodkar
Sri Aurobindo Ashram, Pondicherry
[Untitled Landscape], c. 1948 - 1975
Gelatin Silver Print, 296 x 246 mm
ACP: D2004.82.0012

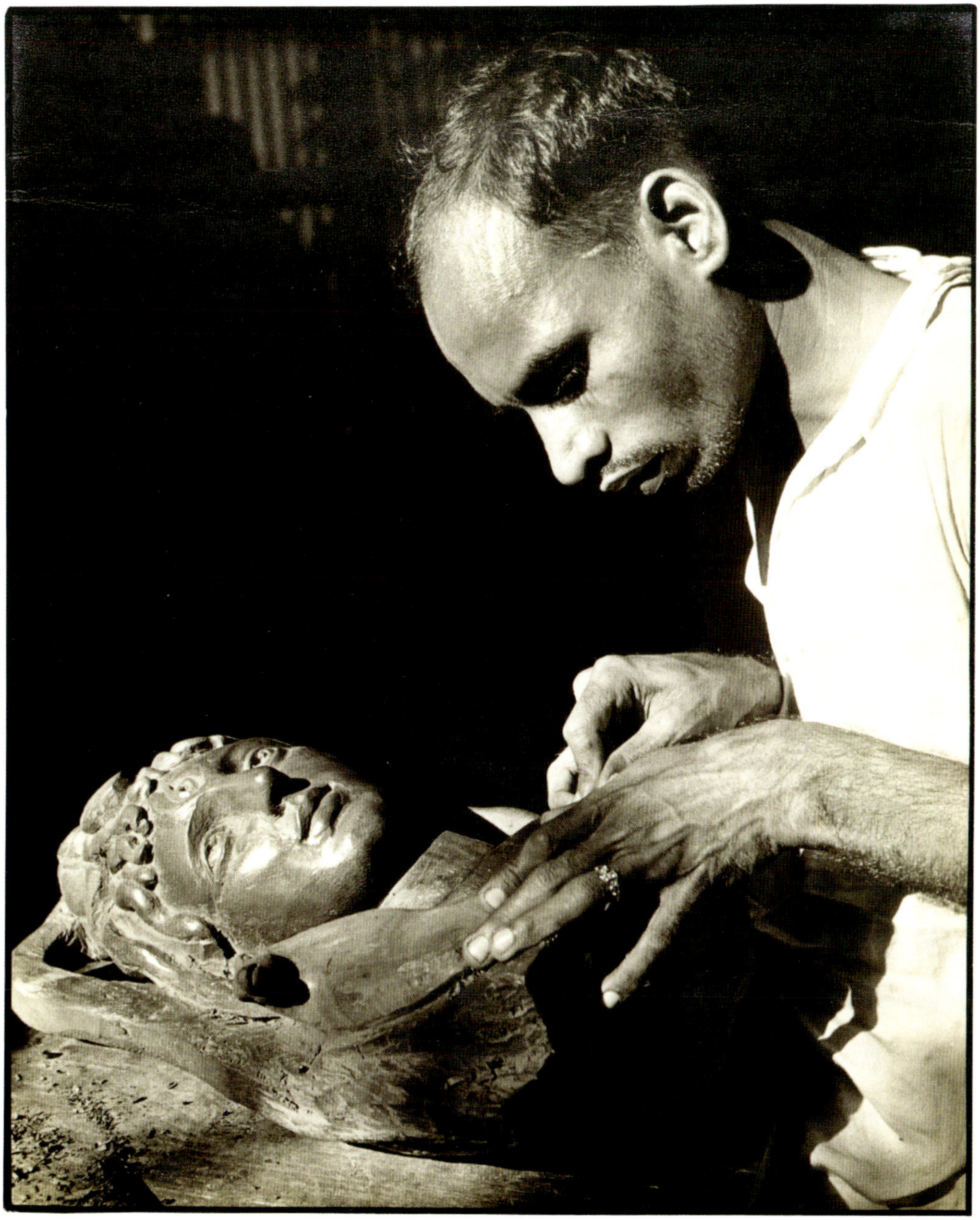

Venkatesh Shirodkar
Sri Aurobindo Ashram, Pondicherry
"Creation," c. 1948 - 1975
Gelatin Silver Print, 291 x 240 mm
ACP: D2004.82.0013

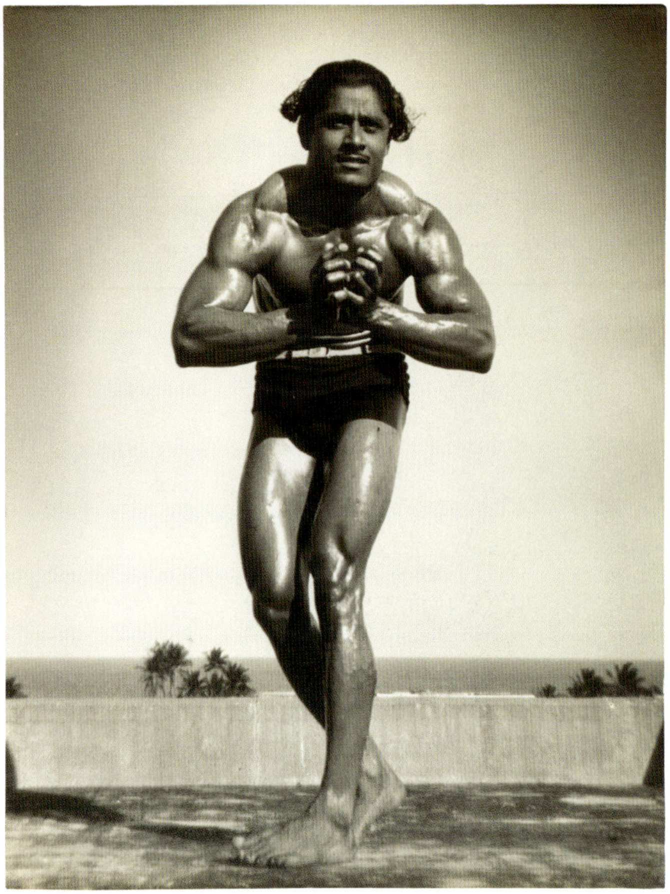

Venkatesh Shirodkar
Photographic Department,
Sri Aurobindo Ashram, Pondicherry
"Mr Asia," c. 1948 - 1975
Gelatin Silver Print, 297 x 228 mm
ACP: D2004.82.0027

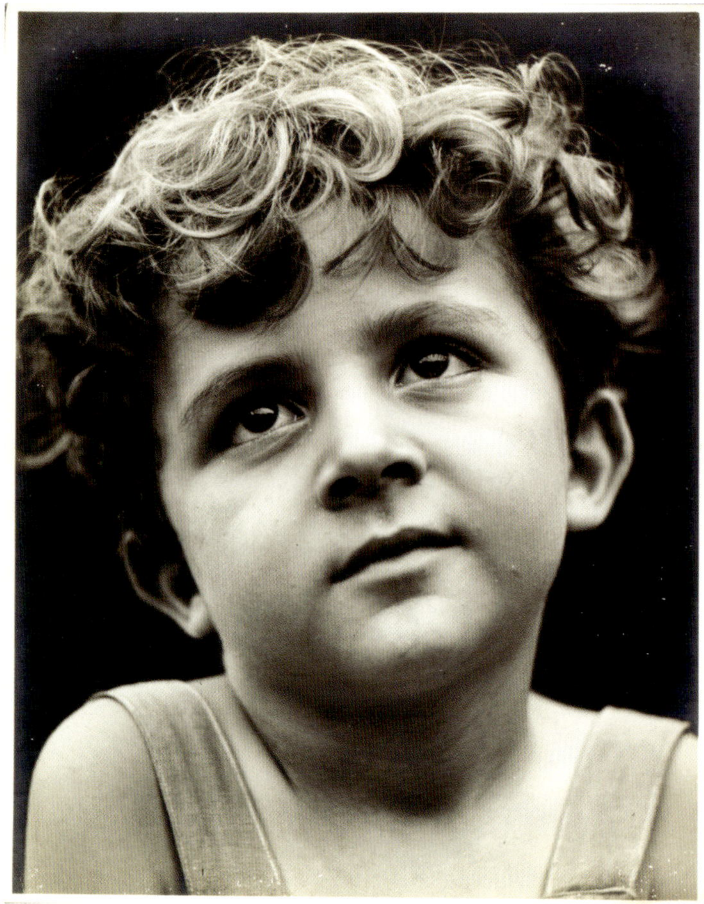

Venkatesh Shirodkar
Sri Aurobindo Ashram, Pondicherry
[Untitled Portrait], c. 1948 - 1975
Gelatin Silver Print, 377 x 303 mm
ACP: D2004.82.0042

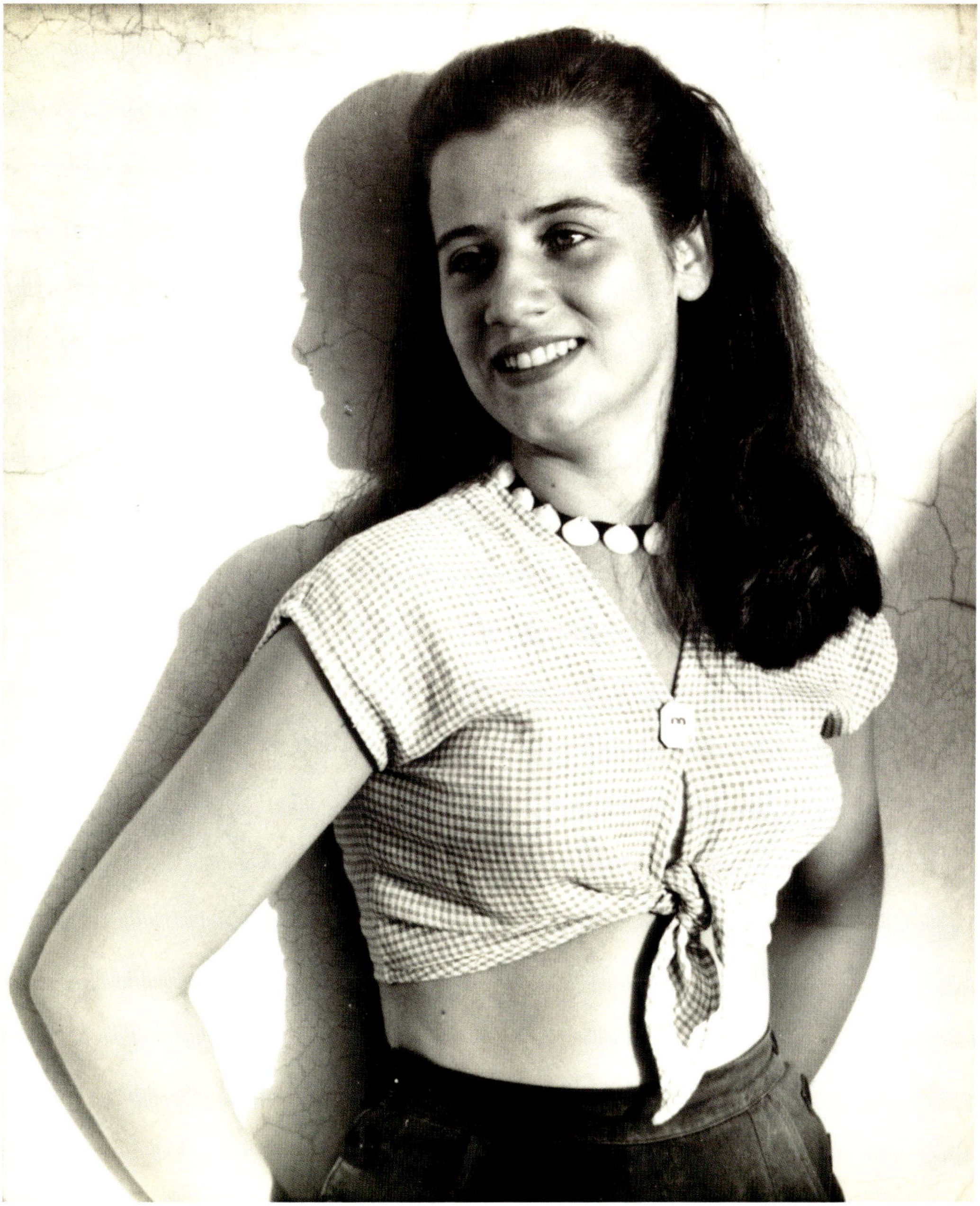

Venkatesh Shirodkar
Sri Aurobindo Ashram, Pondicherry
[Untitled Portrait], c. 1948 - 1975,
Gelatin Silver Print, 286 x 240 mm
ACP: D2004.82.0017

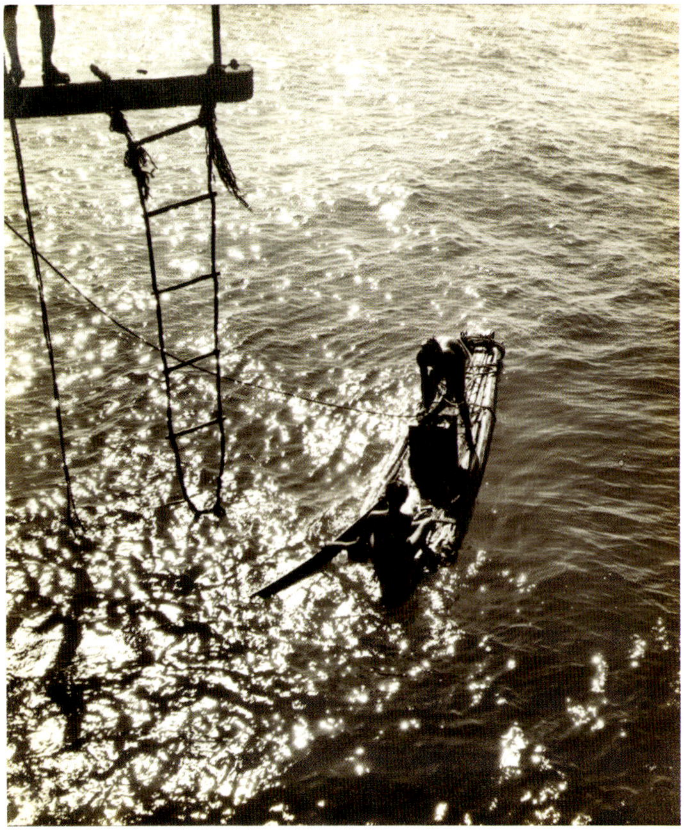

Venkatesh Shirodkar
Sri Aurobindo Ashram, Pondicherry
[Untitled], c. 1948 - 1975
Gelatin Silver Print, 341 x 293 mm
ACP: D2004.82.0040

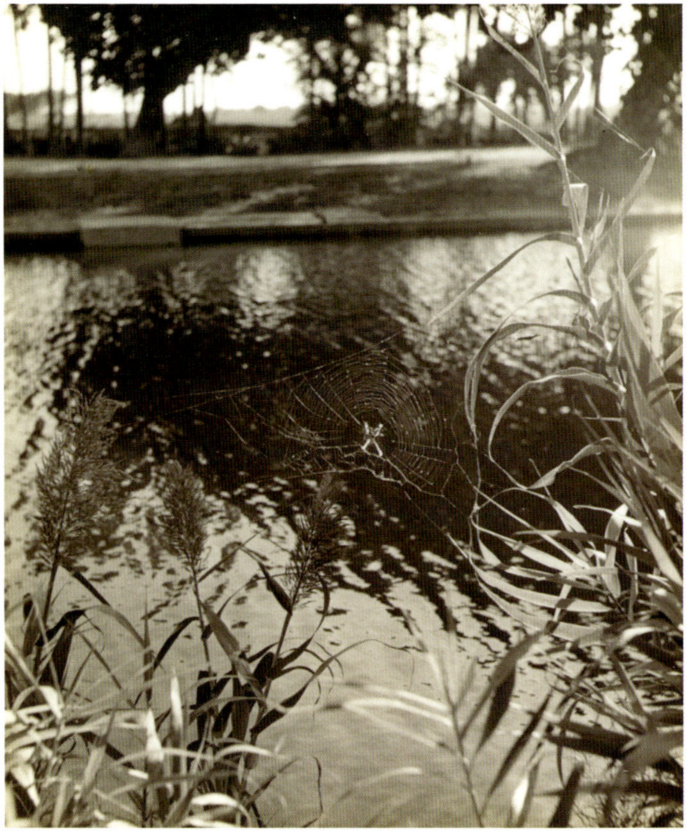

Venkatesh Shirodkar
Sri Aurobindo Ashram, Pondicherry
[Untitled], c. 1948 - 1975
Gelatin Silver Print, 341 x 293 mm
ACP: D2004.82.0040

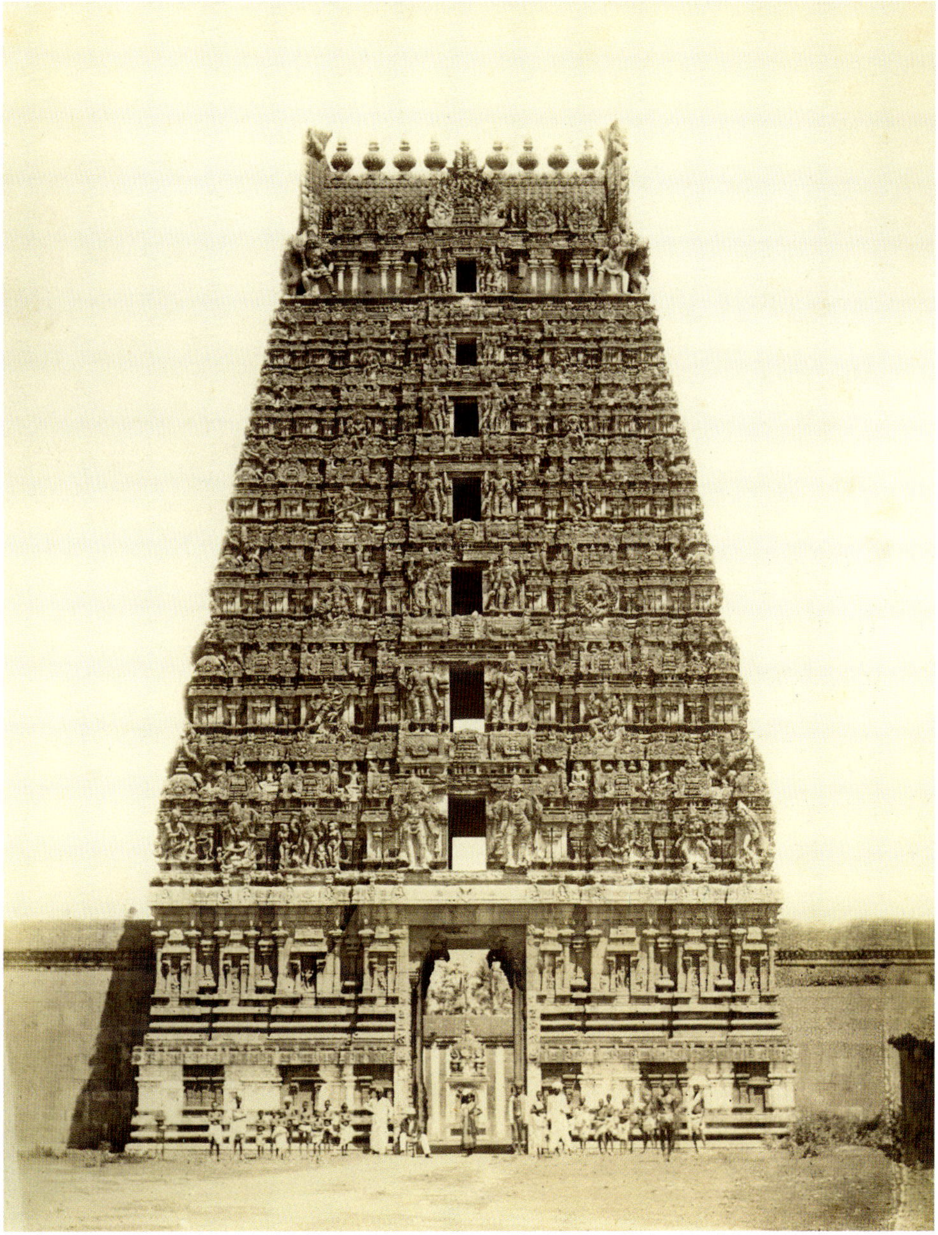

C. (possibly Charles) Moyne
49.Pagode de Vilnour, Porte Principale.
Environs de Pondichery.
(Sri Gokilambal Thirukameshwar Temple, Main Pagoda), c. 1860, Albumen Print, 204 x 162 mm
ACP: 2008.01.0041

The *Sri Gokilambal Thirukameshwar* Temple is located 10 km away from Pondicherry, in Villianur. The temple dates back to the Chola period (12th century) and is dedicated to Shiva. The Pagoda of this temple has a seven-tiered structure. ('Pagoda' is a generic term in the English language referring to any tiered structure). The temple of Villanur was a prominent destination for sightseeing at Pondicherry.

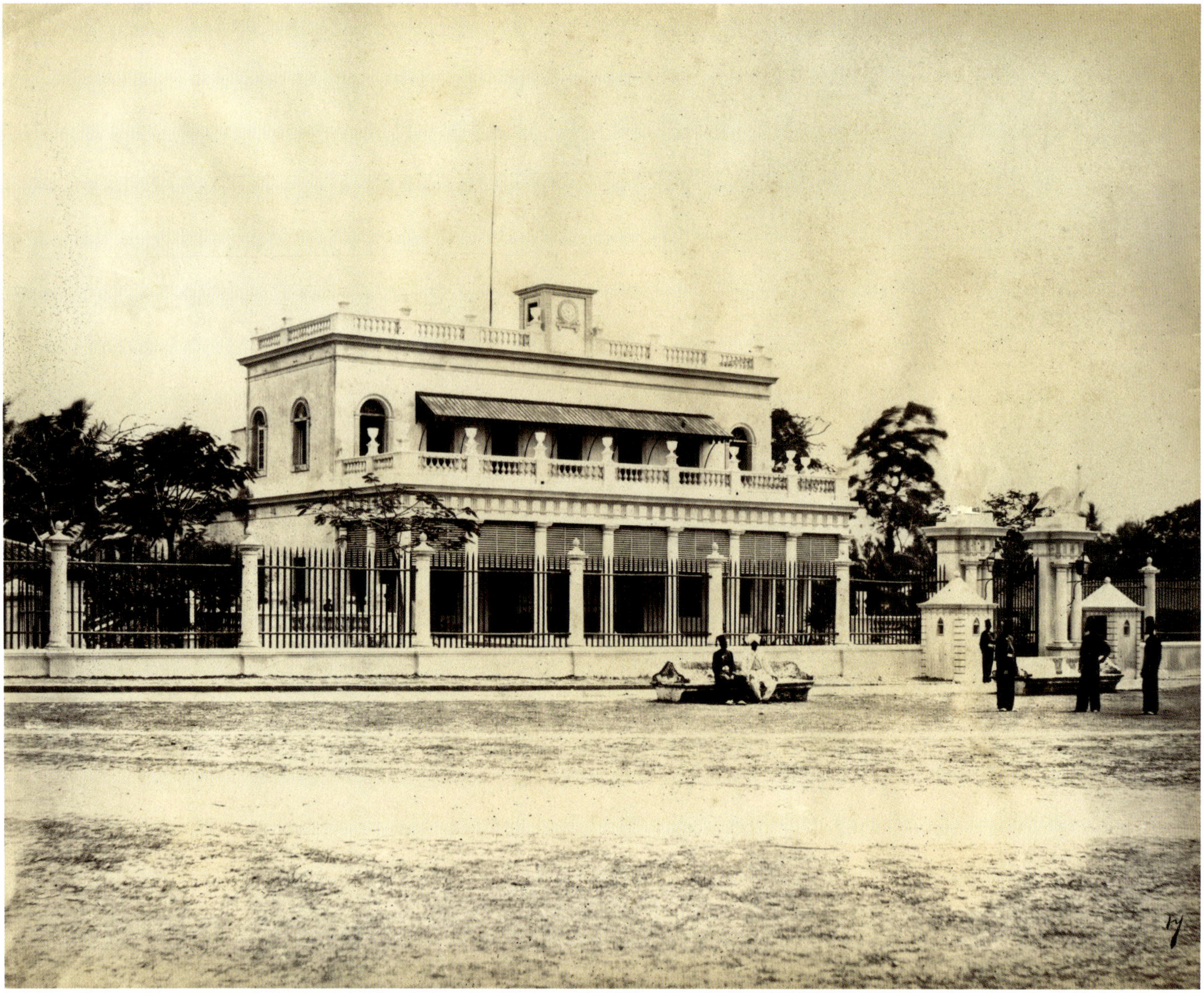

Unknown Photographer
Government House, Karical (currently Karaikal), c. 1860, Albumen Print, Photographer's Ref. 7, 193 x 241 mm
ACP: 97.16.0079(0031)

In 1739, the French took possession of Karaikal, then under the control of Raja Pratap Singh of Tanjore. By a treaty signed in 1750, Pratap Singh ceded 80 villages around Karaikal to the French. Passing under British control after 1761, they were handed over to the French in 1816, and remained in their possession till 1954.

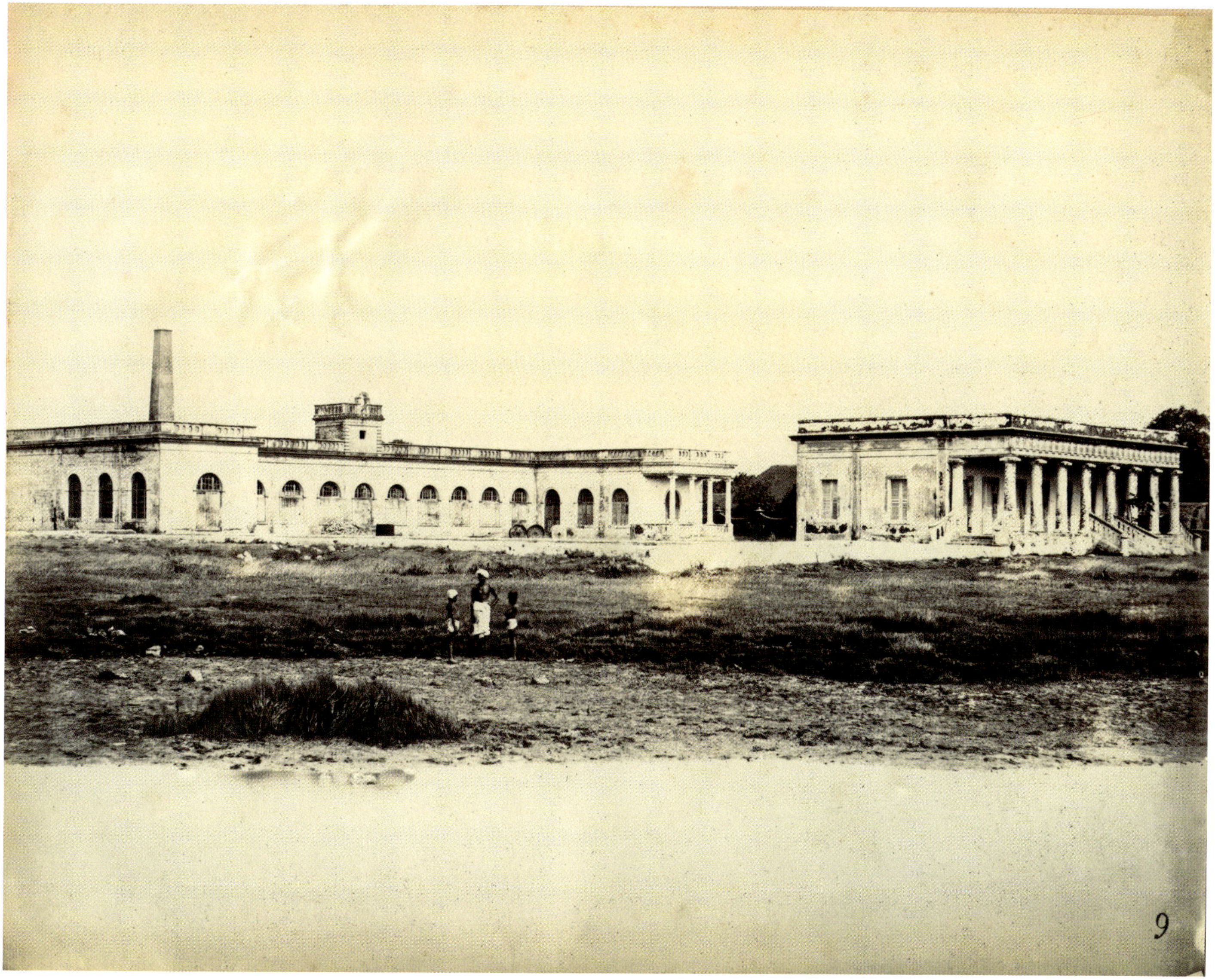

Unknown Photographer
Oil Factory. Karical (currently Karaikal), c. 1860,
Albumen Print, Photographer's Ref. 9,
188 x 241 mm
ACP: 97.16.0079(0057)

Karaikal was the industrial hub in Pondicherry.

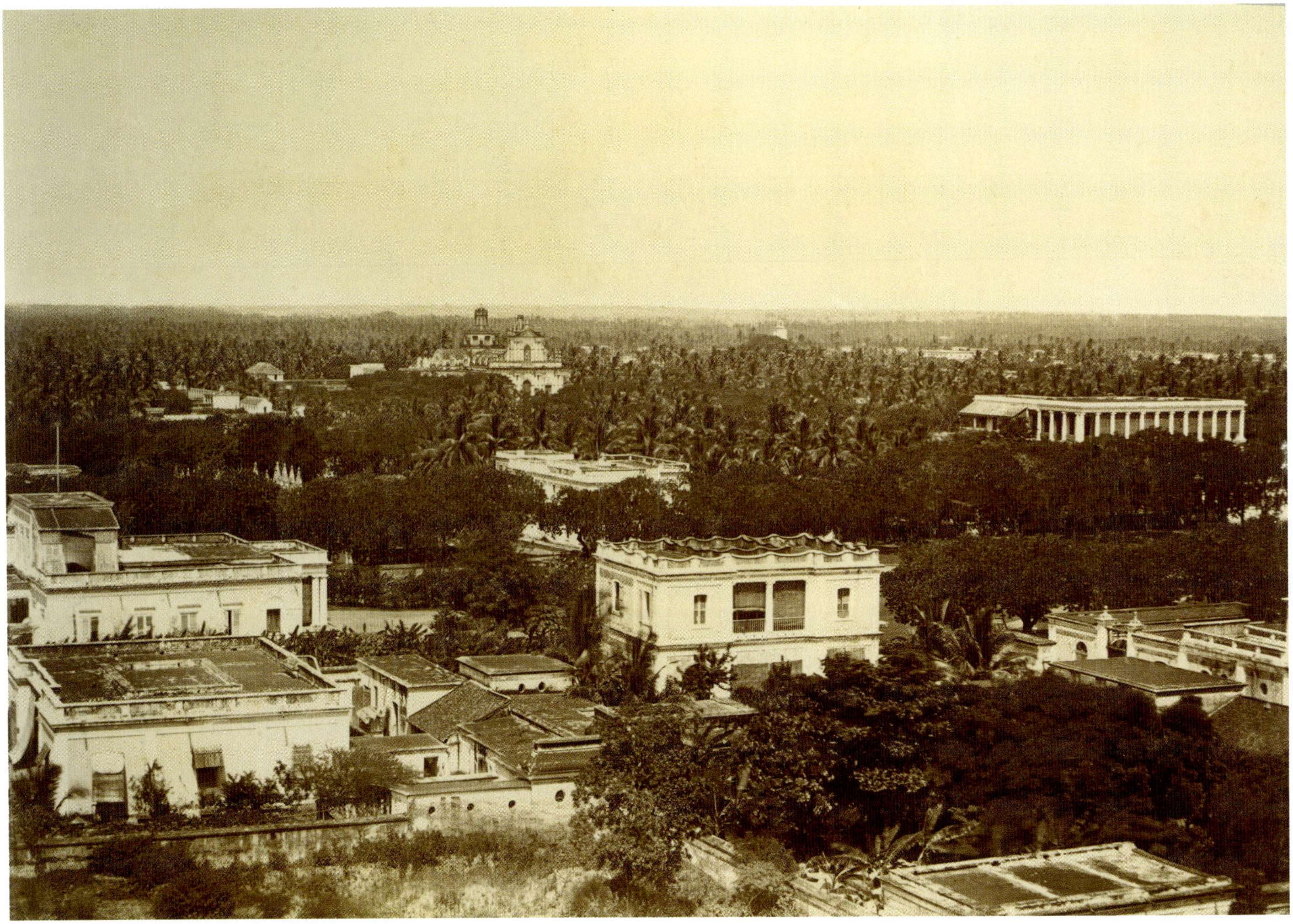

Unknown Photographer
Pondicherry showing Cathedral of the Immaculate Conception in the background, c. 1880,
Albumen Print, 153 x 218 mm
ACP: 95.0033(0061)

The cathedral was built in 1692, with the financial support of Louis XIV, King of France, and was destroyed three times: in 1693 by the Dutch; around 1730; in 1761 by the British. The church was re-built each time at the same site.

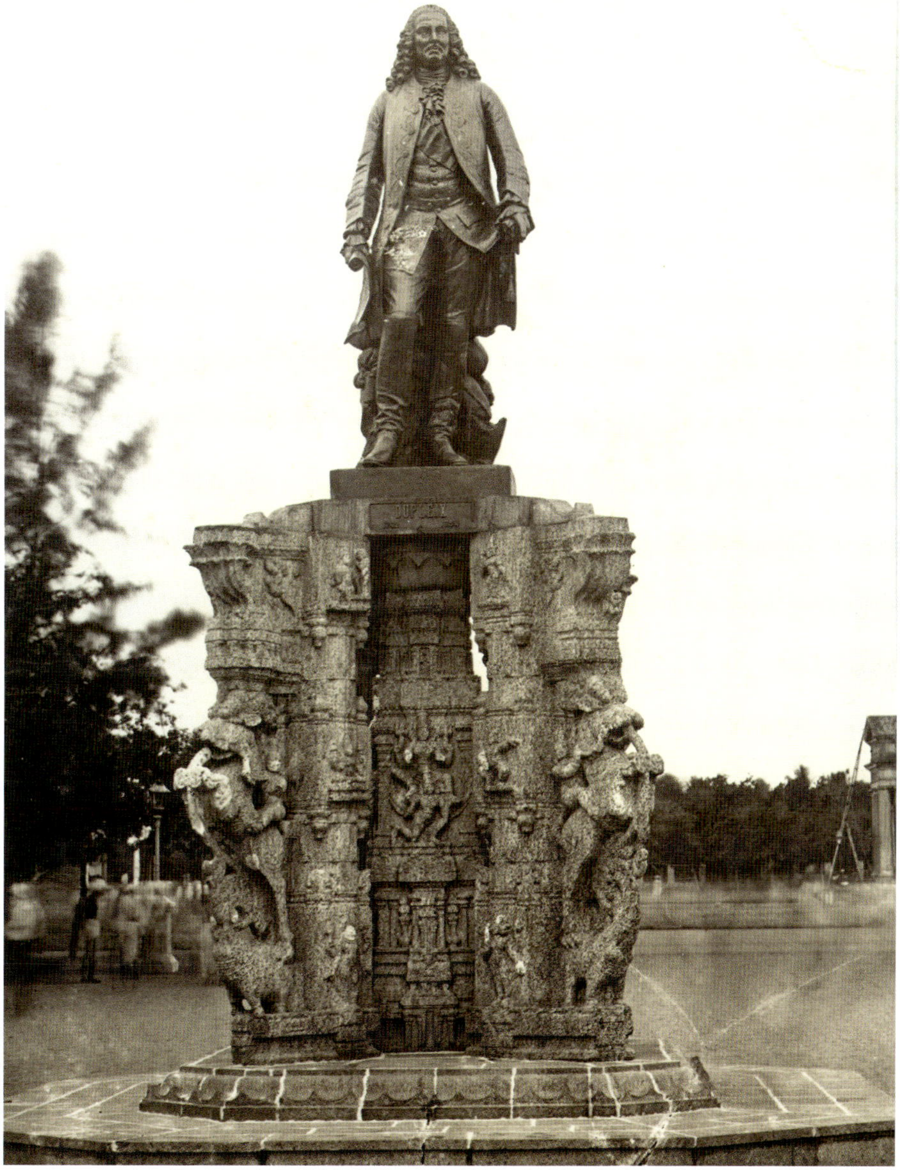

Unknown Photographer
Statue of Dupleix, Pondichery, c. 1880
Albumen Print, 198 x 150 mm
ACP: 95.0033(0062)

Dupleix Monument stands as testimony to the immense contribution made by Joseph-François Dupleix (1697-1763), Governor-General of Pondicherry (r.1742-54), in trying to consolidate French supremacy in some parts of India, along with building and expanding the city of Pondicherry. The statue, which is 2.88 metres tall stood on a pedestal constructed from monolithic pillars of temples brought from nearby Gingee Fort.

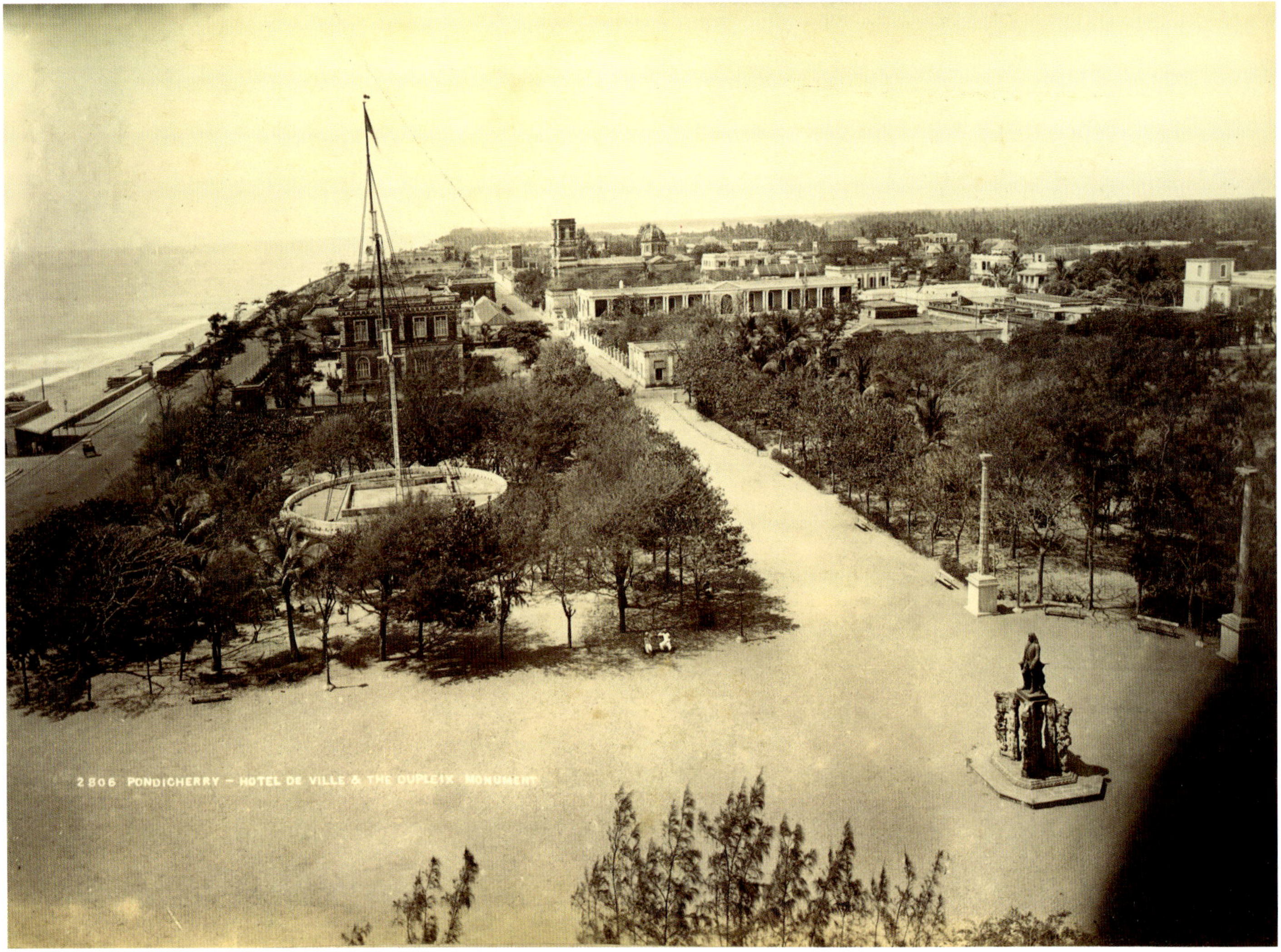

Bourne & Shepherd
Pondicherry- Hotel de Ville & the Dupleix monument, c. 1890, Albumen Print, Photographer's Ref. 2806, 212 x 284 mm
ACP: 95.0015(0002)

The Hôtel-de-Ville (Town Hall), a symbol of French colonial power, was built in 1870. It was the first large administrative building to be constructed after more than 100 years of French rule in the city of Pondicherry. The Dupleix Monument can also be seen in the foreground, which is the statue of Joseph-François Dupleix (1697-1763), Governor-General of Pondicherry (r.1742-54), who played a significant role in making Pondicherry a prime French settlement in India.

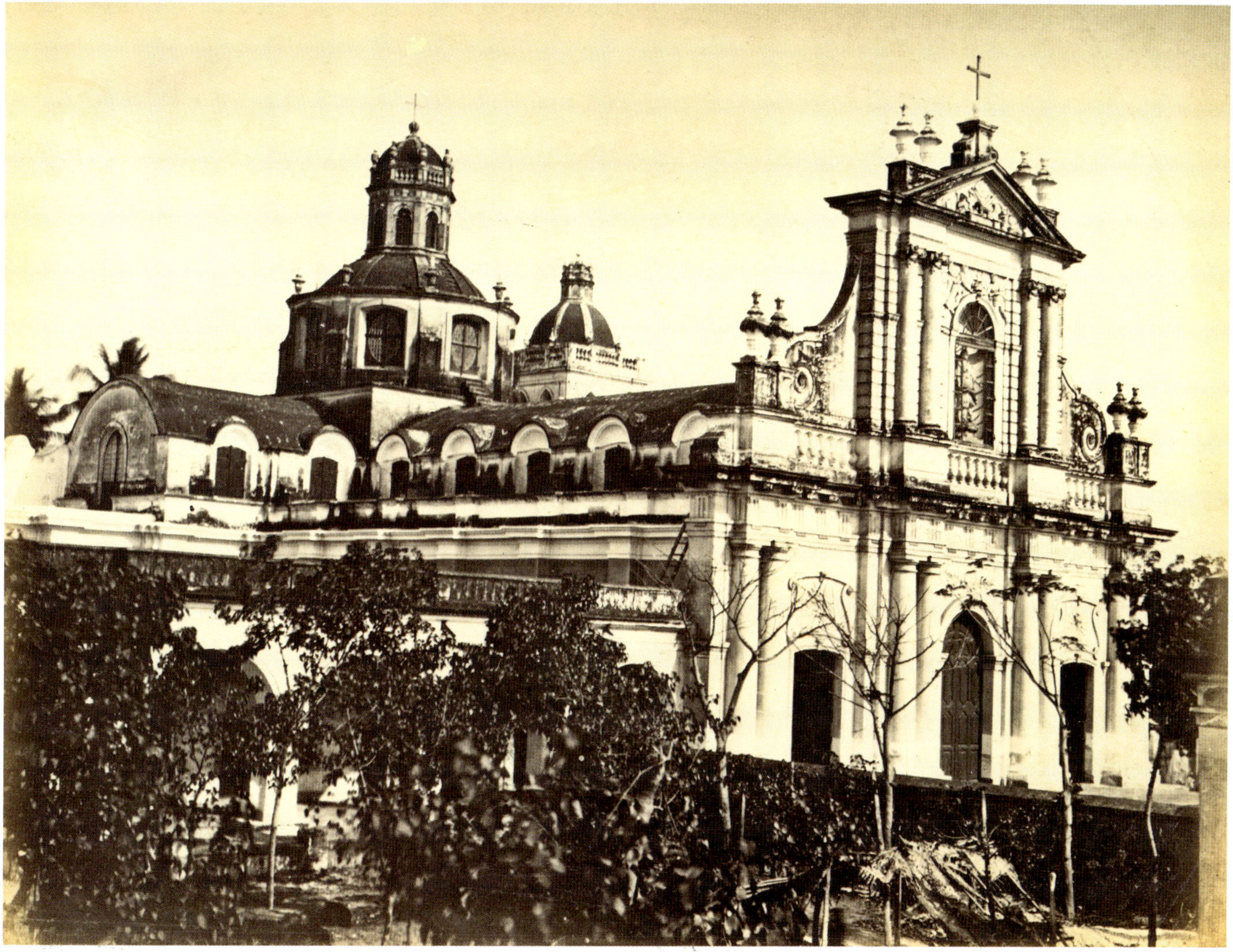

C. (possibly Charles) Moyne
Eglise de la Mission Opus (Cathedral of The Immaculate Conception), c. 1860, Albumen Print, 180 x 237 mm
ACP: 97.52.0001(0026)

The Cathedral of The Immaculate Conception was built in 1692, with the financial support of Louis XIV, King of France, and destroyed three times. The architecture of the cathedral was inspired by the Val-de-Grâce Church in Paris.

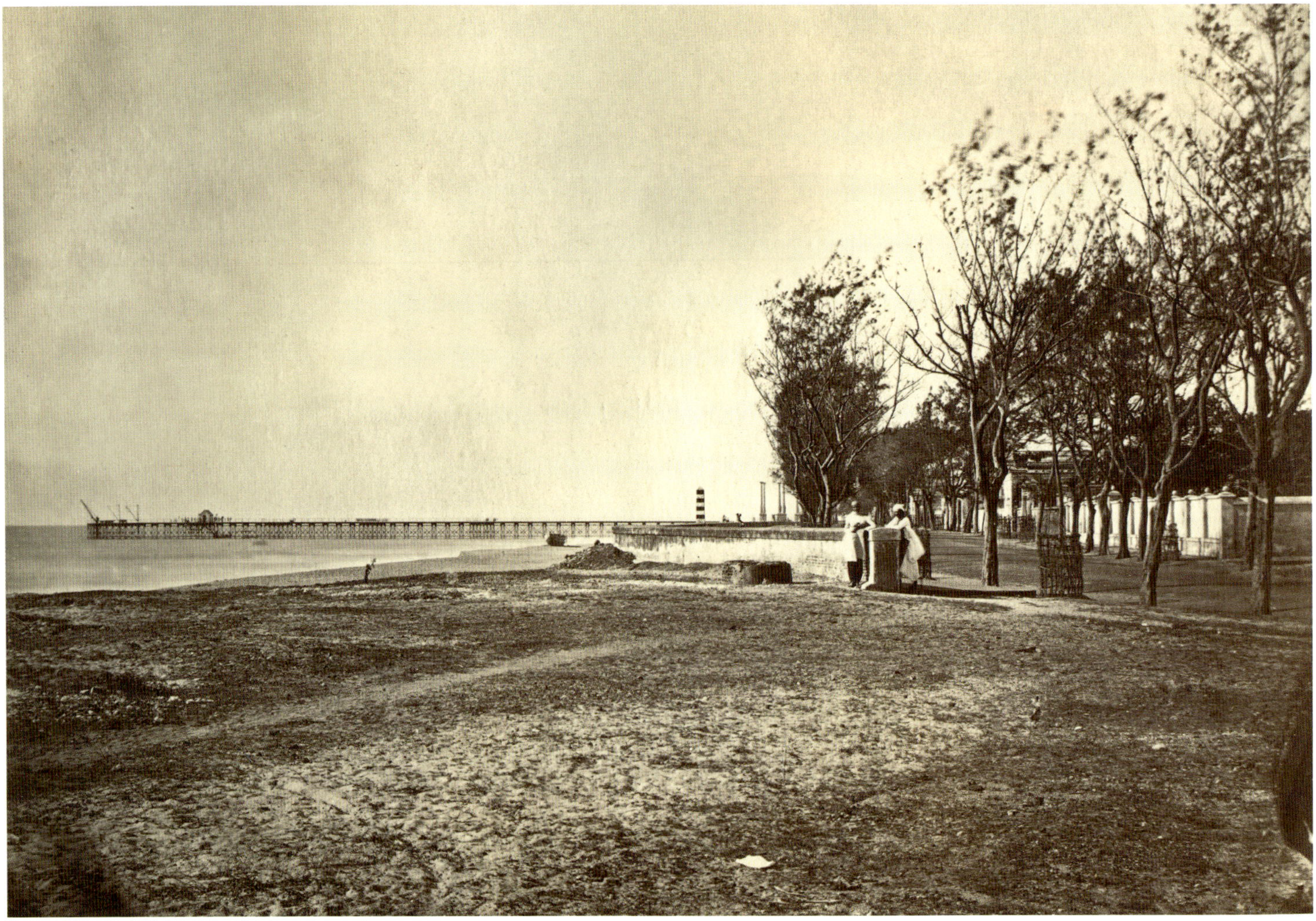

Unknown Photographer
The pier Pondichery E. Indies (Pondicherry, The Pier), c. 1880, Albumen Print, 152 x 221 mm
ACP: 97.48.0001(0038)

As Pondicherry became an important trading port, a 192 metre long iron pier was built by colonial engineer, Lamairesse (who also built the Government Square Fountain). Inaugurated on 15 August 1866, it was extended twice, in 1881 and in 1908, covering a final distance of 336 metres. A cyclone in 1952 destroyed the pier and a new one was erected in 1963.

This pier was used for the transportation of goods from the cargo boats to the shore and the godowns.

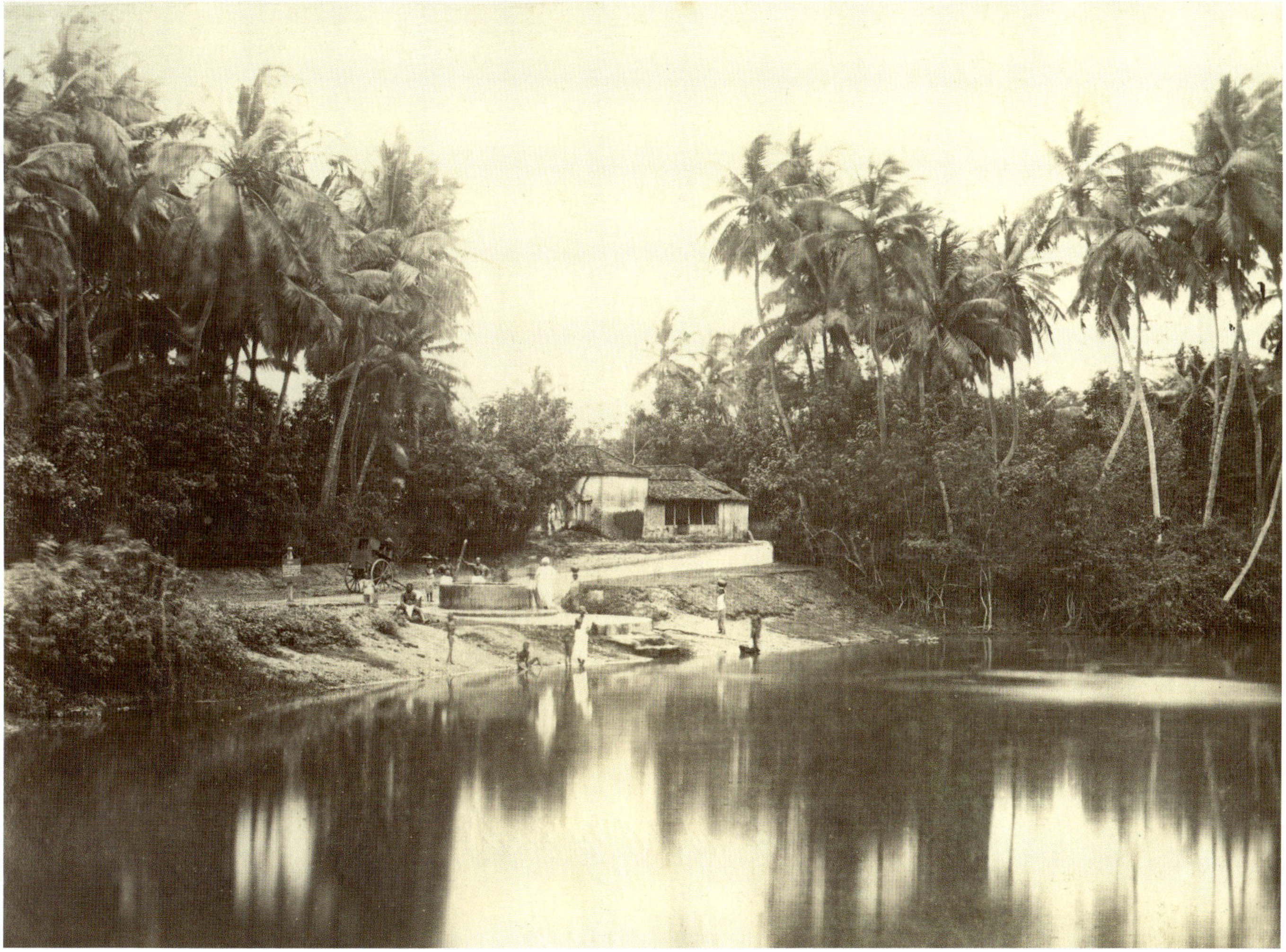

Unknown Photographer
Tank for supplying Pondichery with water,
c. 1880, Albumen Print, 154 x 213 mm
ACP: 97.48.0001(0039)

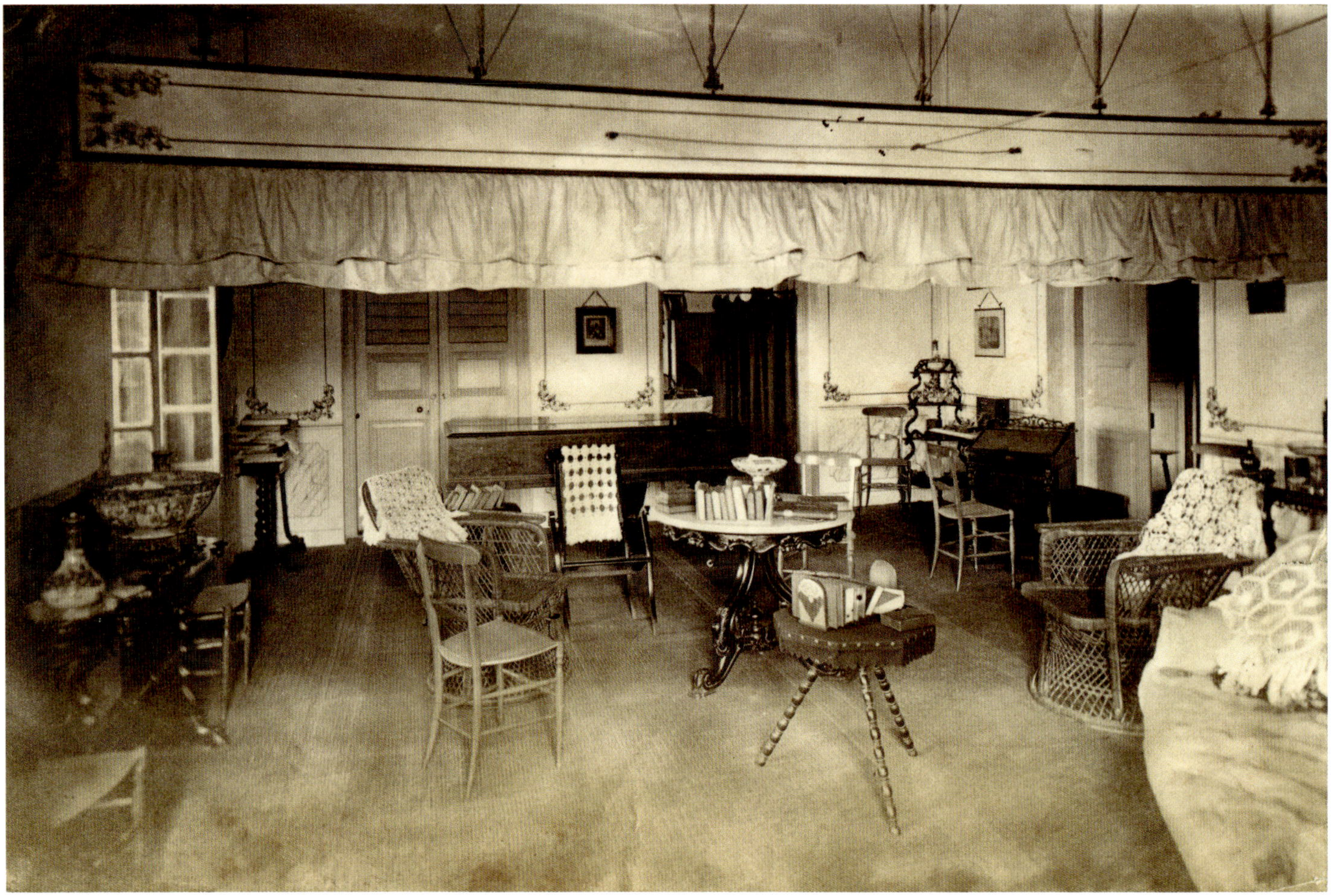

Unknown Photographer
Interior in Pondicherry
(Pondicherry: Interior of European Home),
1895, Albumen Print, 102 x 155 mm
ACP: 96.20.0157

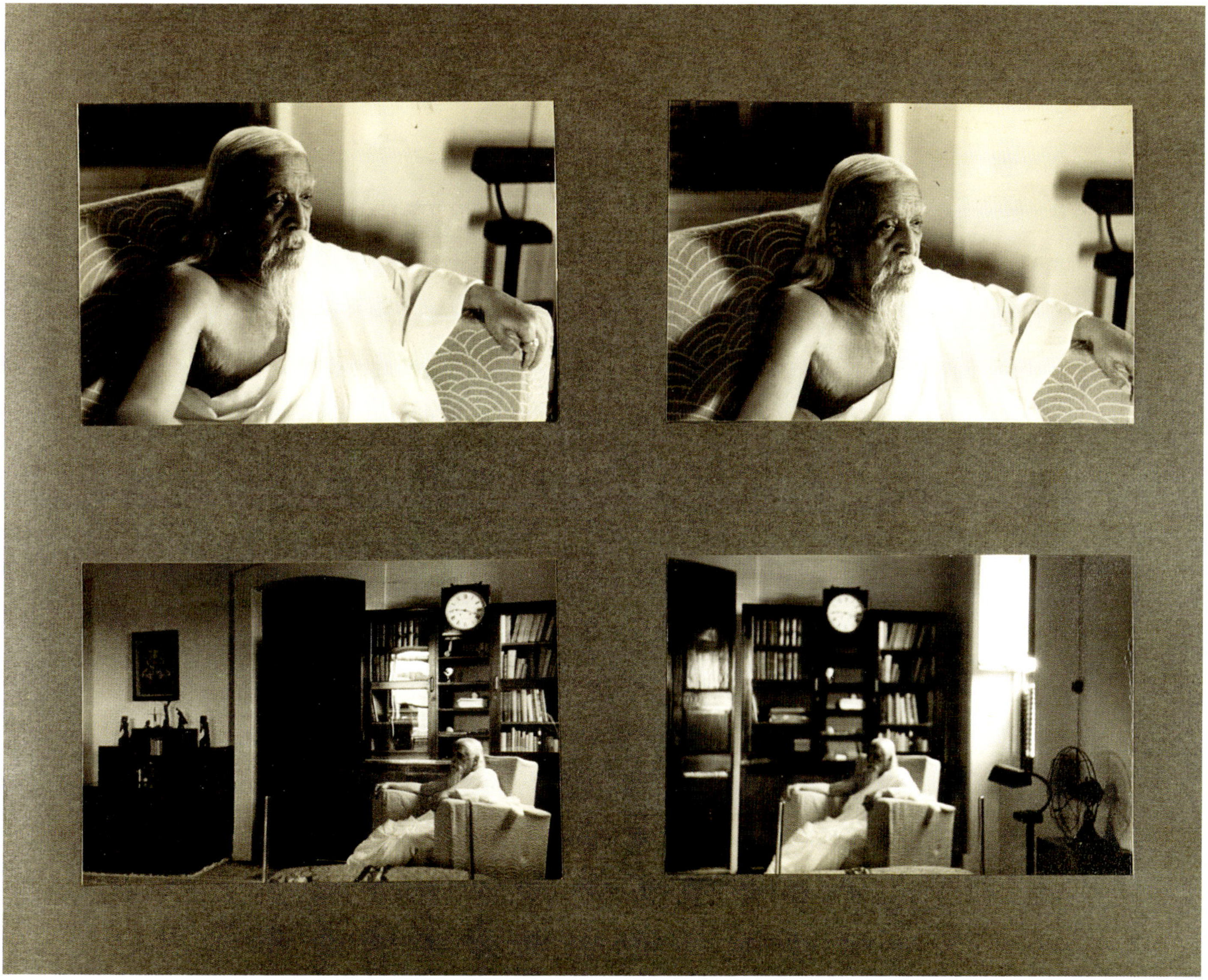

Henri Cartier-Bresson
Sri Aurobindo Ghosh from the album 'Sri Aurobindo and His Ashram,' April 1950, Gelatin Silver Prints, 315 x 403 mm
ACP: D2005.06.0001(0014-17)

Personal Notes by Henri Cartier-Bresson as provided by the Henri Cartier-Bresson Foundation, Paris: 762.
The morning after darshan, I went to thank Mother to have let me take their pix at the darshan, but I told her that the conditions of light there would make the results most unsatisfactory to the disciples who were expecting a portrait as clear as the one in circulation now. She told me that was what they wanted from me: some indistinguishable shadow of themselves and in this I had fully succeeded. Mother was so helpful and she convinced Aurobindo and I came in his bedroom with my camera. The room was so neat and tidy and so impersonal: dark wood furniture, waxed big arm chair – everything seemed right out of a large furniture magazine. The only thing that was on the bed spread across was the inevitable tiger skin, which seems to be the companion of any one trying or achieve spiritual realisation. The old man did not wink an eye for the 10 minutes I was watching him. He did not seem to belong to that impersonal setting, yet he was entrenched in his chair.

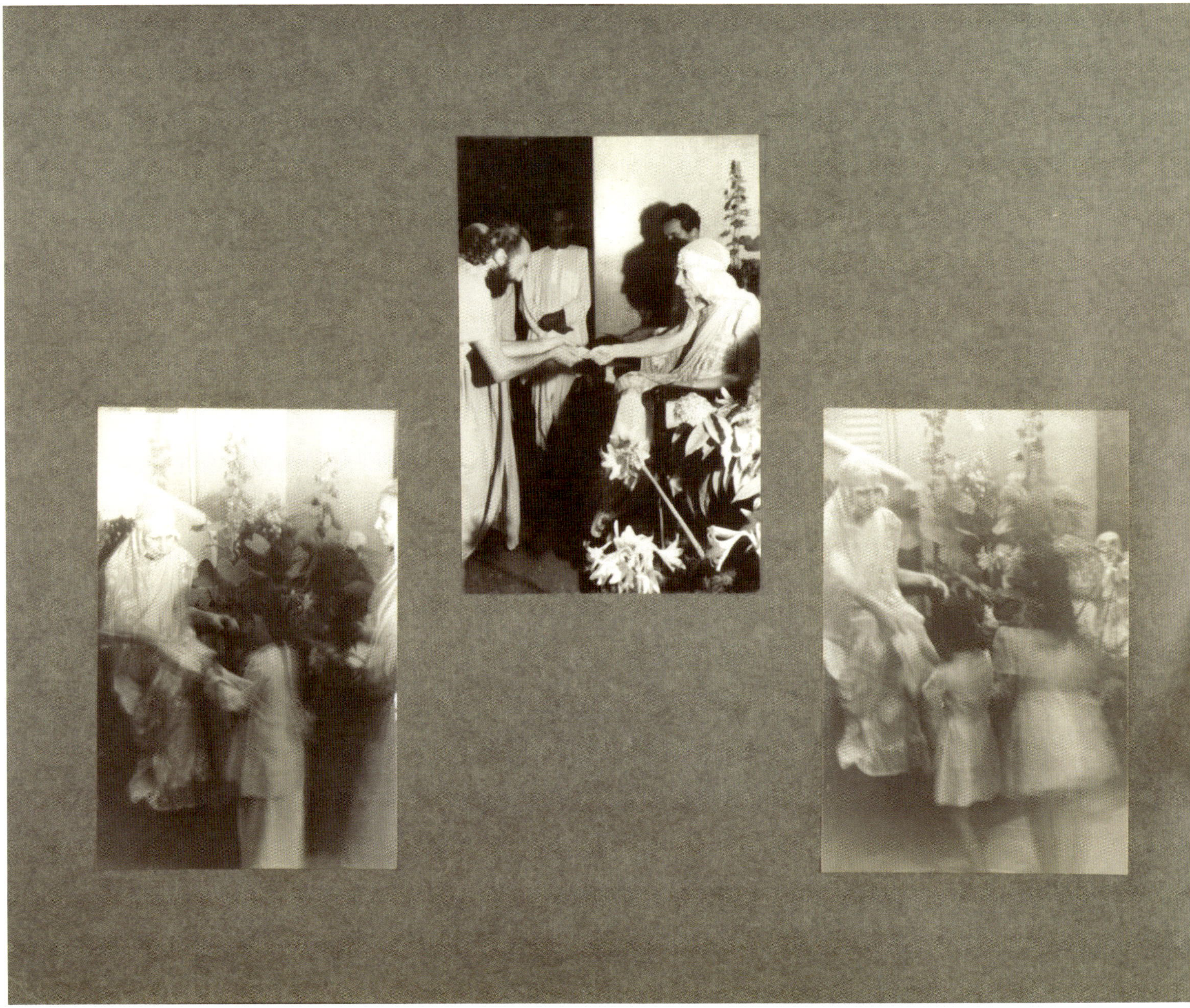

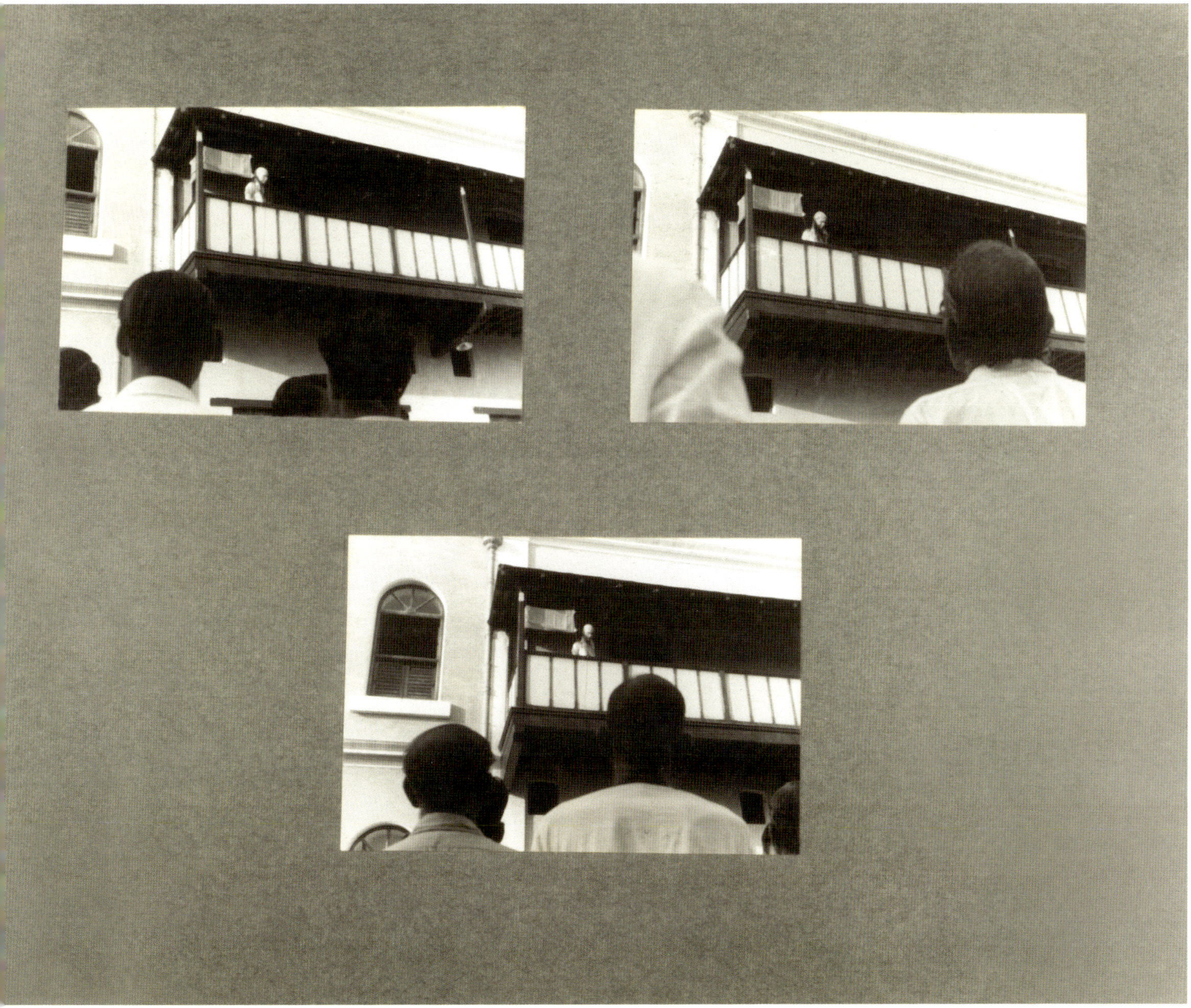

Henri Cartier-Bresson
[Left: The Mother at the daily ritual of receiving devotees. Right: The Mother giving *darshan* to her devotees early morning from her verandah] from the album 'Sri Aurobindo and His Ashram,'
April 1950, Gelatin Silver Prints, 403 x 315 mm (each)
ACP: D2005.06.0001 (0026-0031)

759-42 [Right-hand side] from Bresson's personal diary
The first ritual of the day takes place at 6:45 am when Mother appears on the balcony of the Ashram. She turns her head from left to right which gives her time to see exactly who is gathered in the street below. Then she slips back inside, silent as an apparition.

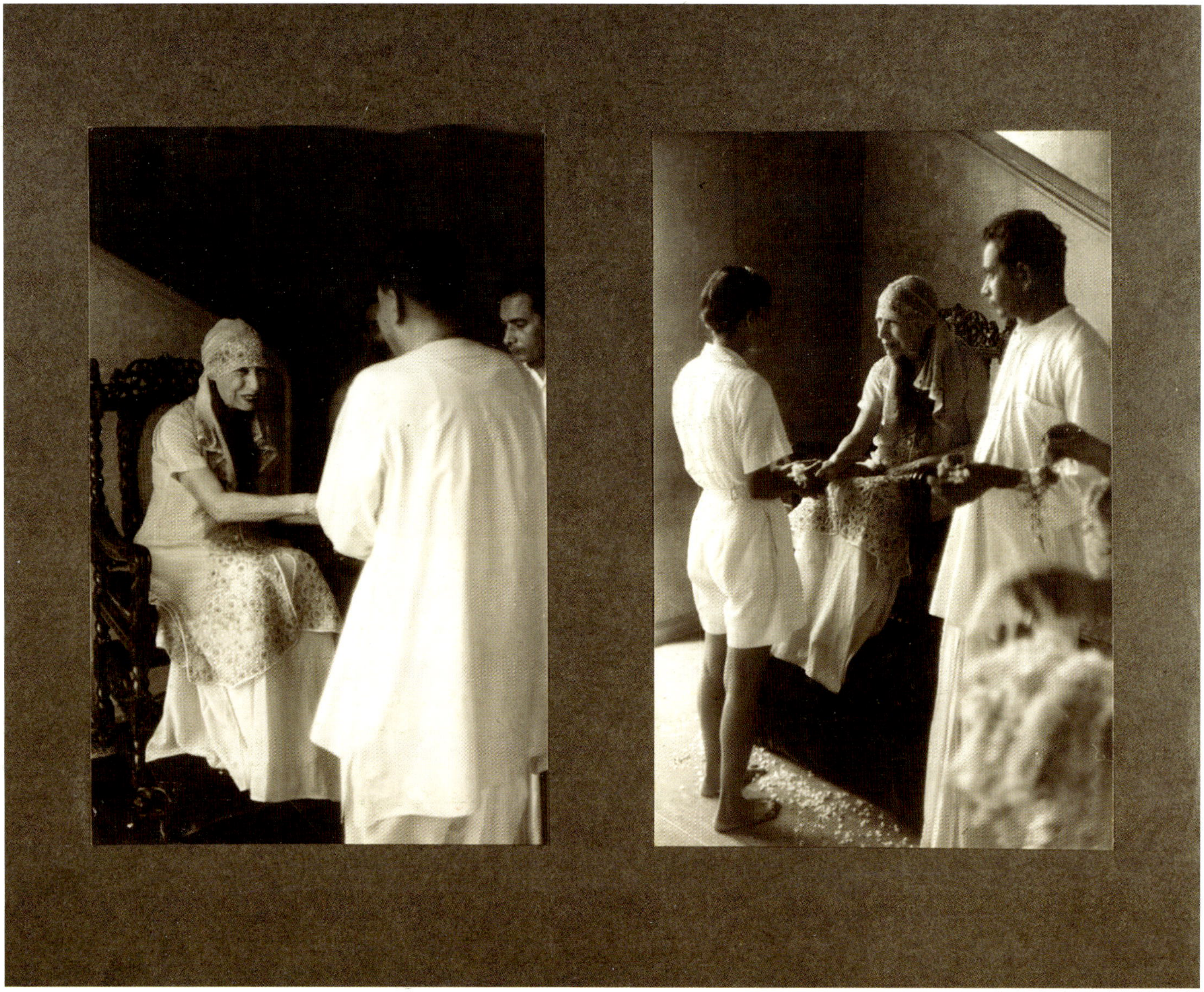

Henri Cartier-Bresson
[The Mother at the daily ritual of receiving devotees] from the album 'Sri Aurobindo and His Ashram,' April 1950
Gelatin Silver Prints, 315 x 403 mm
ACP: D2005.06.0001 (0036-0037)

761-1 from Bresson's personal diary
Part of the daily ritual around Mother is the exchange of flowers, each of which has a special meaning. Mother receives little bouquets and for a very close disciple, or an especially deserving one, she will select one flower and hand it over to him, often accompanied by one of her deep seraphic smiles.

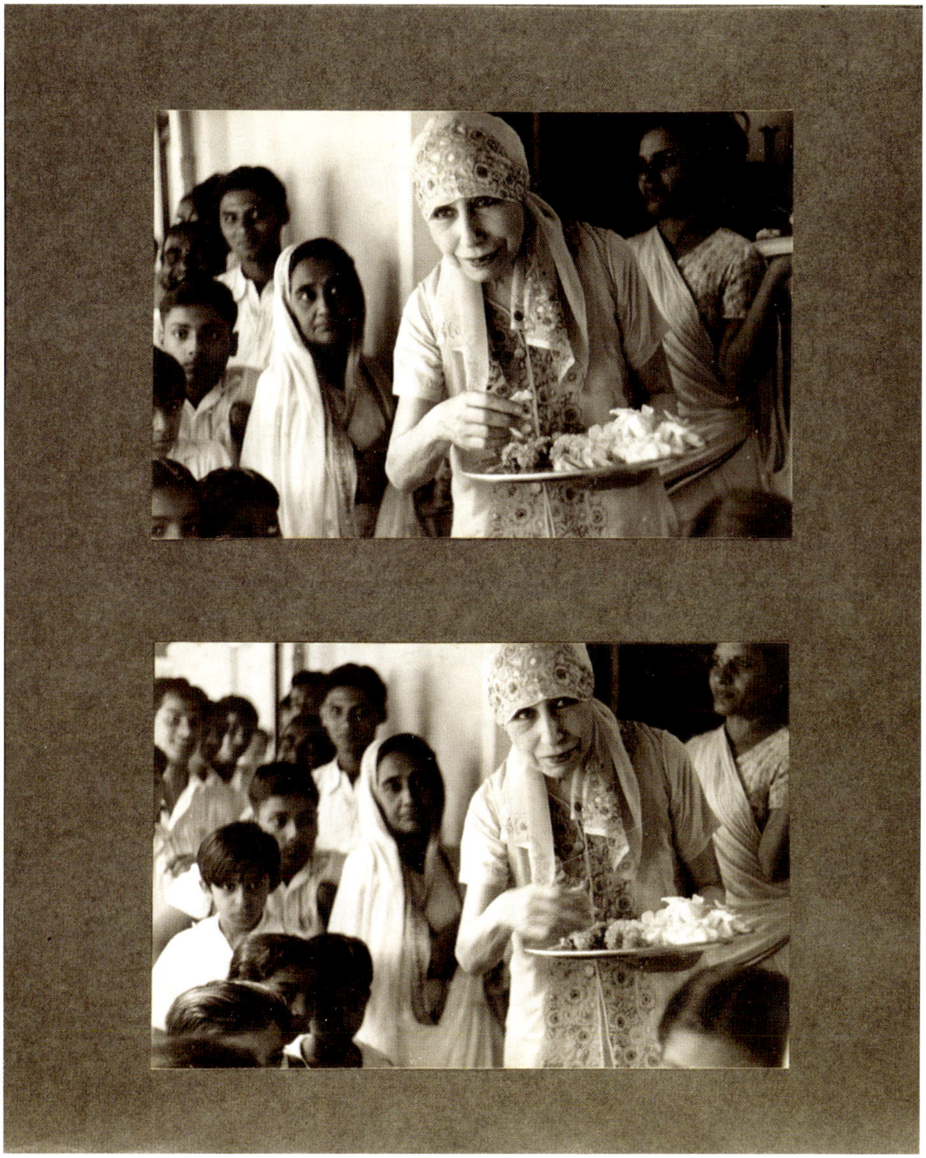

Henri Cartier-Bresson
[The Mother at the daily ritual of throwing flowers at the devotees] from the album 'Sri Aurobindo and His Ashram,' April 1950, Gelatin Silver Prints, 403 x 315 mm
ACP: D2005.06.0001 (0055-56)

763-2 from Bresson's personal diary
Every day after lunch Mother comes down to the inner courtyard of the Ashram. At that time she throws flowers to her disciples, which they catch in flight.

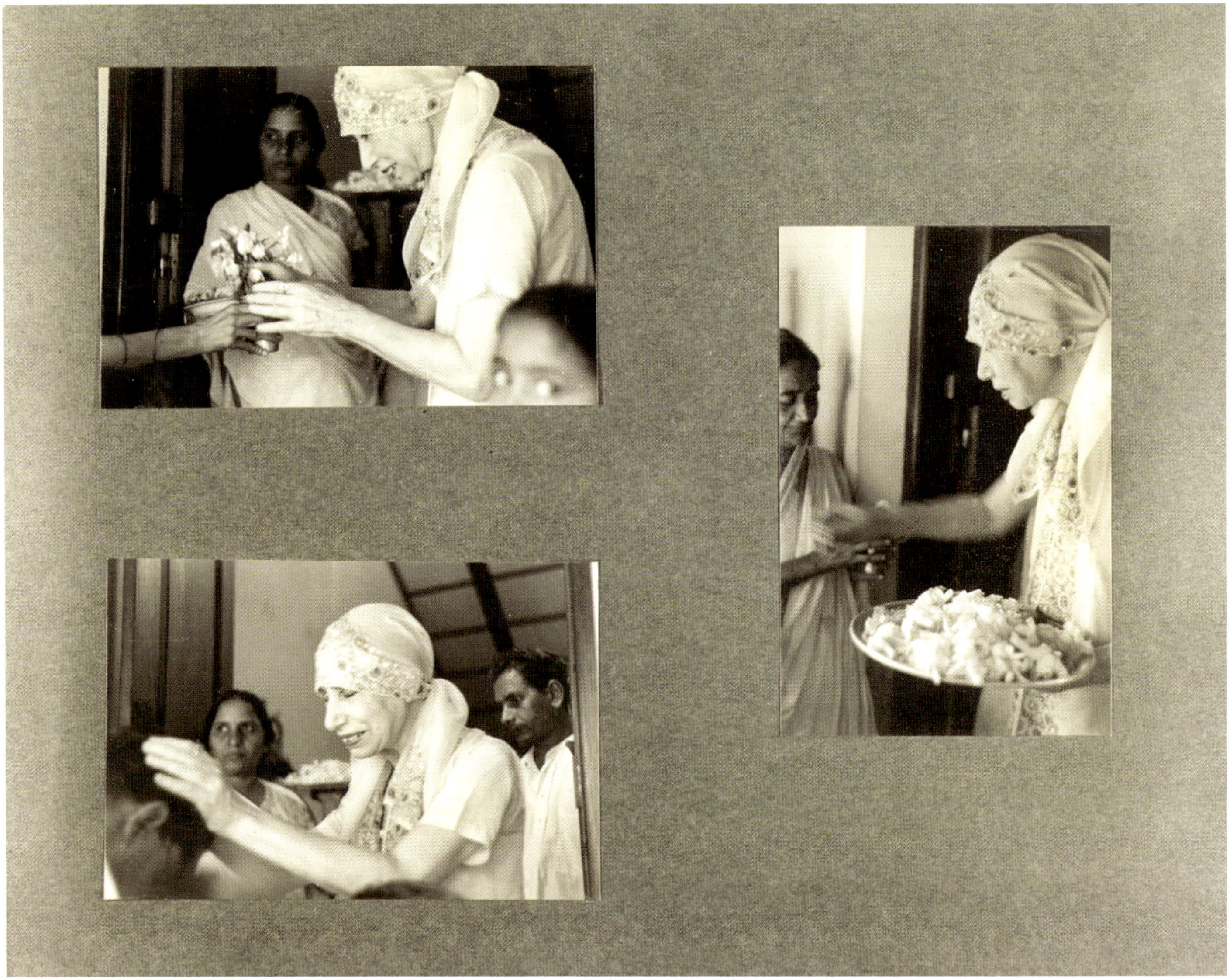

Henri Cartier-Bresson
[The Mother at the daily ritual of throwing flowers at the devotees and meeting people] from the album 'Sri Aurobindo and His Ashram,' April 1950, Gelatin Silver Prints, 403 x 315 mm
ACP: D2005.06.0001 (0060-62)

Personal Notes by Henri Cartier-Bresson as provided by the Henri Cartier-Bresson Foundation, Paris: 755.
I forgot mentioning the Bull of the Ashram, they have also about 30 cows but as it is far from enough for the consumption, they buy milk from the villagers but the villagers must bring their cows to be milked in the ashram shed under their supervision to get a guarantee of cleanliness. I also took pix in one of the farms of the Ashram. They perform irrigation in the traditional manner, but they also have an engine to pump water. The cost of the Ashram is Rs 4000 a day. The Ashram promised me to directly send me figures on the different aspects, (number of men, women, children, cost, significance given to different flowers).

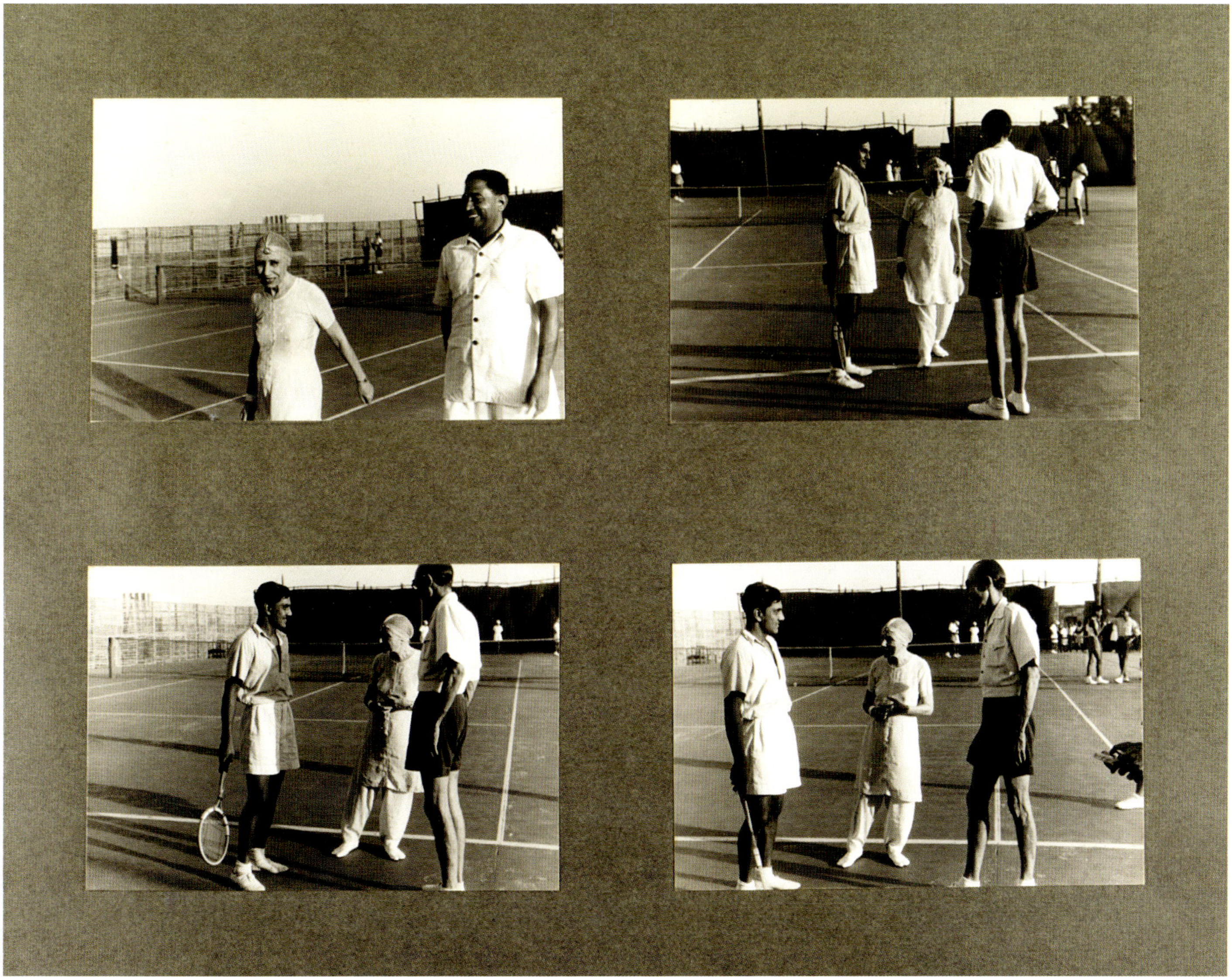

Henri Cartier-Bresson
[The Mother warming up to play tennis] from the album 'Sri Aurobindo and His Ashram,' April 1950, Gelatin Silver Prints, 315 x 403 mm
ACP: D2005.06.0001 (0075-0078)

765-40 from Bresson's personal diary
Mother on the tennis ground. At left Pranab, a young Bengali who is director of physical culture at the Ashram. He is one of the persons closest to Mother. At right Povitro (meaning purity), Secretary General of the Ashram who has lived there since 1925. He is a mathematician, an ex-student of the Paris Dcole Polytechnique. His real name is de Saint-Hilaire.

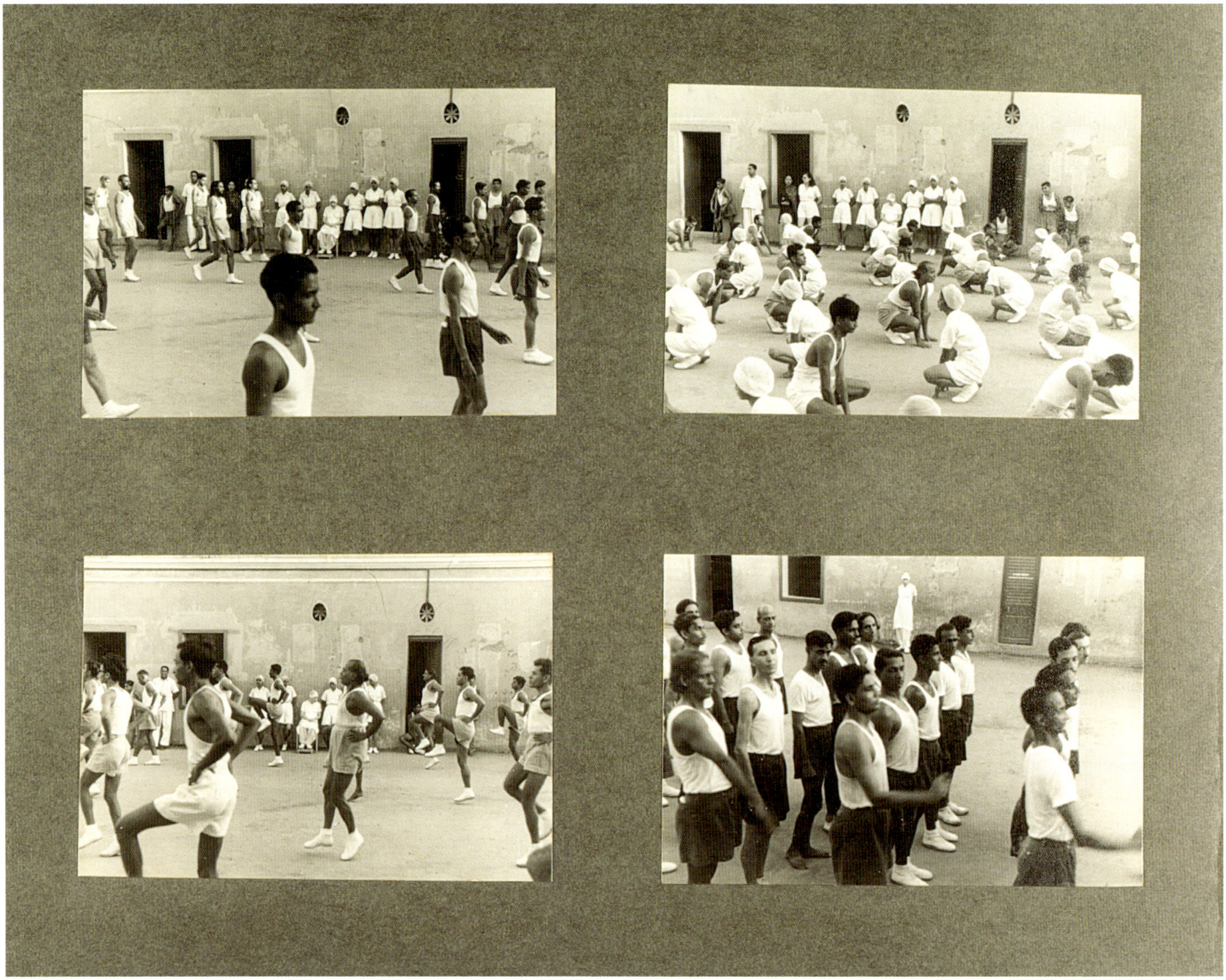

Henri Cartier-Bresson
[Daily physical education activities at the Ashram] from the album 'Sri Aurobindo and His Ashram,' April 1950, Gelatin Silver Prints, 315 x 403 mm
ACP: D2005.06.0001 (0085-0088)

Personal Notes by Henri Cartier-Bresson as provided by the Henri Cartier-Bresson Foundation, Paris: 757-41.
Physical training is an important part of the spiritual education disciples receive at the Ashram. Every afternoon Mother herself watches the exercises on the Ashram's playground. These pictures showing Mother in the background were the first Cartier-Bresson was allowed to take of her.

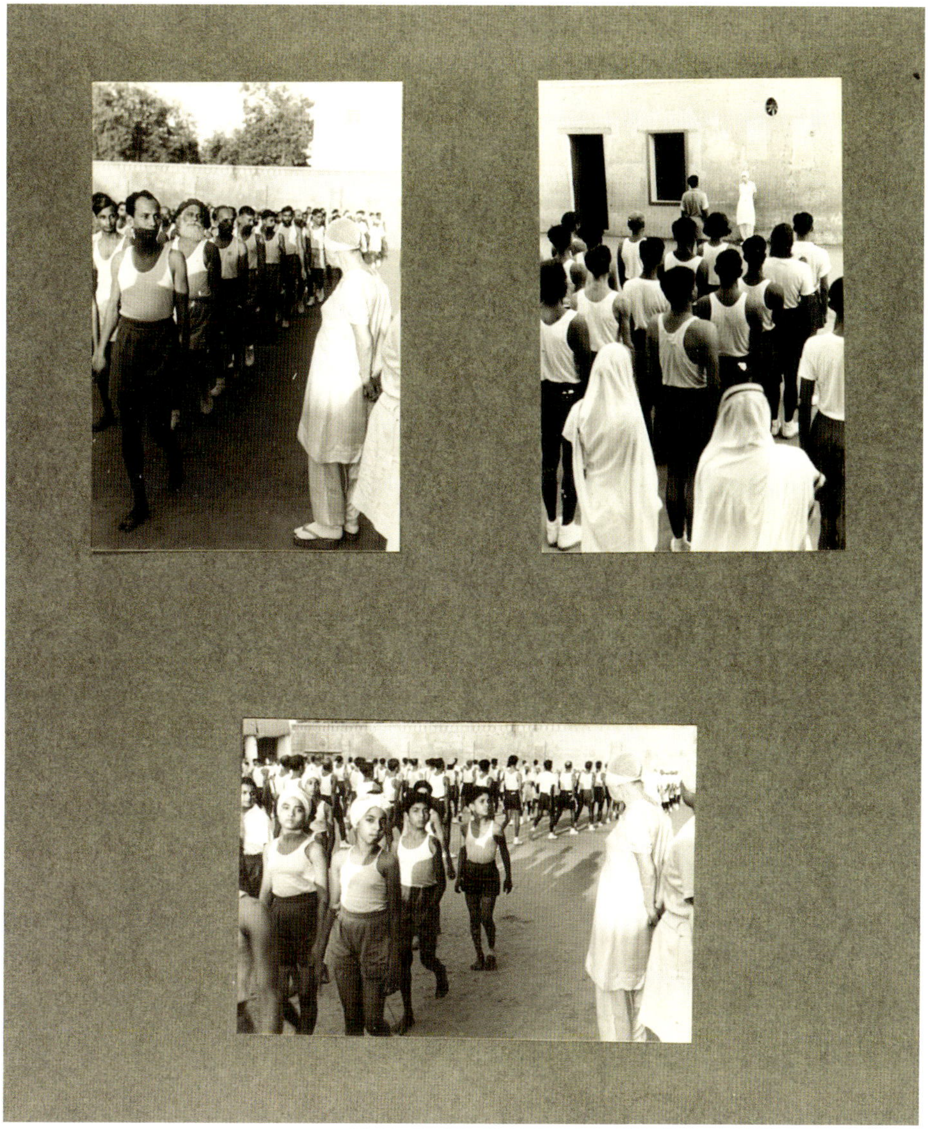

Henri Cartier-Bresson
[Daily physical education activities at the Ashram with the Mother] from the album 'Sri Aurobindo and His Ashram,' April 1950,
Gelatin Silver Prints, 403 x 315 mm
ACP: D2005.06.0001 (0089-0091)

758-36 from Bresson's personal diary
Every day afterthe gymnastic exercises are over, everybody stands at attention for 10 minutes of meditation. Mother stands at the wall of the playground, facing her disciples.

757-39 from Bresson's personal diary
After the exercises, the disciples parade in front of Mother.

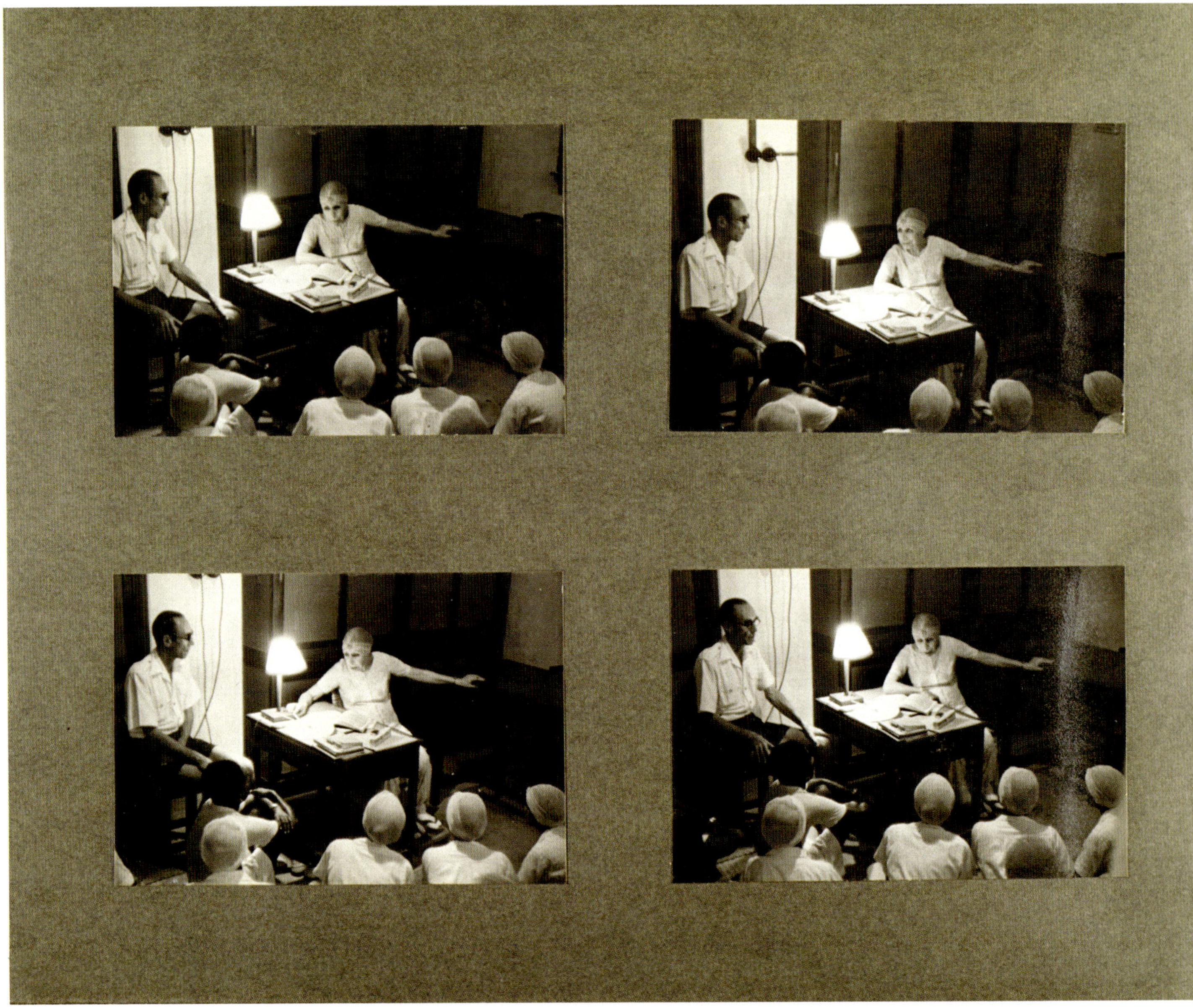

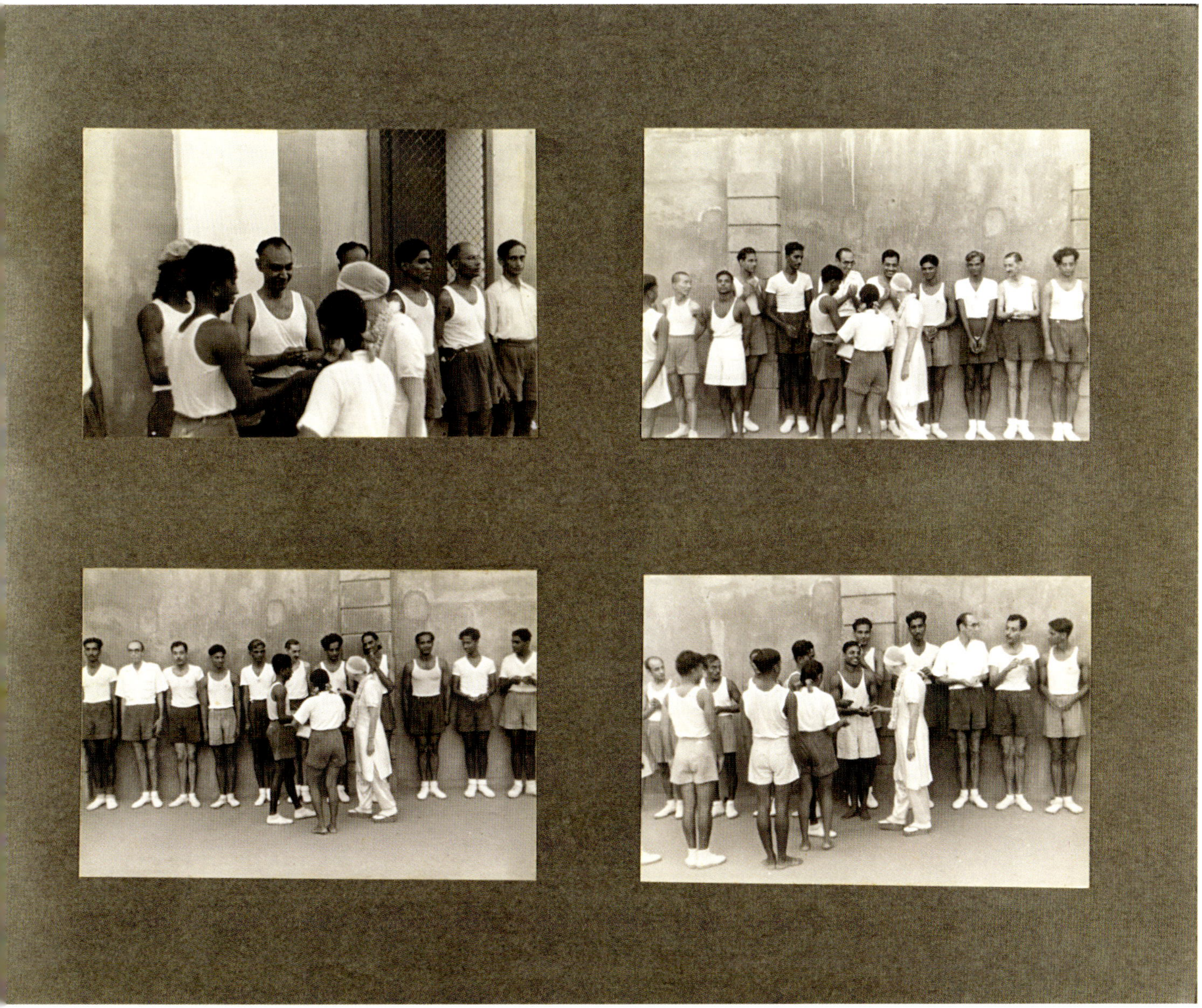

Henri Cartier-Bresson
[Daily activities at the Ashram with the Mother] from the album 'Sri Aurobindo and His Ashram,' April 1950, Gelatin Silver Prints, 315 x 403 mm (each) ACP: D2005.06.0001 (0111-118)

Personal Notes by Henri Cartier-Bresson as provided by the Henri Cartier-Bresson Foundation, Paris: 759.
Quietly the crowd of disciples dispersed to go and have their breakfast in the dining hall 5 or 4 blocks from there on the main square of the town. But this is a great day. One of the 4 great days of the year when Aurobindo appears. Devotees coming from all parts of Bengal, Gujarat and elsewhere (including some foreign devotee who was in Trivanamalai a week before) were in front of the entrance of the Ashram. Pix of devotees passing through the streets on their way to the dining hall. Immediately the disciples of the Ashram paraded in formations, (according to the colour of their pants-shorts) the colour of the shorts show what category they belong to- children, grown ups with little physical training, grown ups taking only little physical training etc...

BRIEF NOTE ON SRI AUROBINDO ASHRAM AND PHOTOGRAPHY

Prof. Kittu Reddy

"Sarvam Khalu idam Brahman"
Verily, all this is Brahmam.

Sri Aurobindo Ashram is an institution dedicated to the practice of Yoga (*sadhana*). We believe that unlike a traditional ashram, the activities here are not engaged in for their own sake. Though there is an immense desire to encourage physical development for the enhancement of a spiritual life, there is also an aesthetic or conceptual thrust inculcated by the notion of *nishkama karma*, or desireless work.

At the Sri Aurobindo International Centre of Education, the students are trained with an integrated bearing, one that considers all aspects of their development and maturing, including physical education in the form of athletics, gymnastics, combative techniques etc.; as well as intellectual training via art-based activities so that the aesthetic development of the student is also nurtured.[1]

We feel that 'Art' must be used to refine and sensitize man's nature. It helps to purify and respond more keenly to a sense of the present, as well as understand 'reality' as opposed to the external composure of things—in all forms of Nature.

In the words of Sri Aurobindo himself, in *The National Value of Art*

> *At a certain stage of human development, the aesthetic sense is of infinite value in this direction. It raises and purifies conduct by instilling a distaste for the coarse desires and passions of the savage, for the rough, uncouth and excessive in action and manner, and restraining both feeling and action by a striving after the decent, the beautiful, the fit and seemly...*
>
> *Plato in his Republic has dealt with extraordinary emphasis on the importance of music in education; as is the music to which a people is accustomed, so, he says in effect, is the character of that people.*
>
> *So wonderfully has God made the world that a man using a simple combination of lines, an unpretentious harmony of colours, can raise this apparently insignificant medium to suggest absolute and profound truths with a perfection which language labours with difficulty to reach.*
>
> *A nation surrounded daily by the beautiful, noble, fine and harmonious becomes that which it is habituated to contemplate and realises the fullness of the expanding Spirit in itself.*[2]

Consequently, all forms of art flourish in the Ashram, encouraged by the Mother and Sri Aurobindo. Sri Aurobindo was a poet and nurtured any number of them in the Ashram. The Mother too was an accomplished artist herself, having studied art systematically at the *Ecole Des Beaux Arts*, Paris. She, in turn, encouraged and trained many artists in the Ashram. "Photography is an art when the photographer is an artist."[3] As stated at the inauguration of *The Federation of Indian Photography*, by The Mother, these words highlight her keen interest in photography as art practice.

In the 1950s, when photography came to be accepted as an art form in India, The Mother initiated photographic activity to a large extent. Photography was organised into a body named *"Ashram Photography"*. This department, in turn, organised the *Pondicherry International Salon of Photography*, which received photographic entries from all over the world. Enthusiasts from more than 25 countries participated in the exhibition. From more than a 1000 entries received, about a 100 of the best were exhibited and a catalogue was printed.[4]

Though there were pioneering photographers such as Bresson who visited the Ashram, The Mother took a deep interest in maintaining her aesthetic sensibilities, often speaking with photographers about their images extensively. Special panels were often exhibited by invitation to famous internationally known photographers, such as portrait photographer Yusuf Karsh of Canada, and Cecil Beaton, the fashion photographer from the United Kingdom.[5]

As seen in the current exhibition, there were several Indian photographers of merit such as Venkatesh, whose artistic talents drew praise from The Mother herself; Robi Ganguli whose photographs were exhibited in International exhibitions, who also served as a member on the panel of judges in photographic exhibitions in the country. He also was responsible for many publications that were brought out by *The Federation of Indian Photography*. Pranab Kumar Bhattacharya and Tara Jauhar, because of their close proximity to The Mother had the opportunity to take innumerable pictures of her. Others included Chimanbhai Patel and Vidyavrata.[6]

Eventually, the Mother even had an art gallery built for the purpose in 1955. It was remodelled in 1980s as a modern exhibition hall.

ENDNOTES

1 http://www.sriaurobindosociety.org.in/subnav/educentr.htm

2 Ghosh, Aurobindo and Manoj Das, *The Hour of God: Selections from His Writings*. New Delhi: Sri Aurobindo Ashram Trust and Sahitya Akademi. 1995

3 The Mother, On Education (Volume 12, Collected Works of the Mother, Sri Aurobindo Ashram, Pondicherry, Second Edition 2002), pg 241.

4 For further readings, Sri Aurobindo Ashram Archives can be contacted.

5 Ibid.

6 As narrated by Robi Ganguli (b. 1932), a photographer residing in the Ashram.

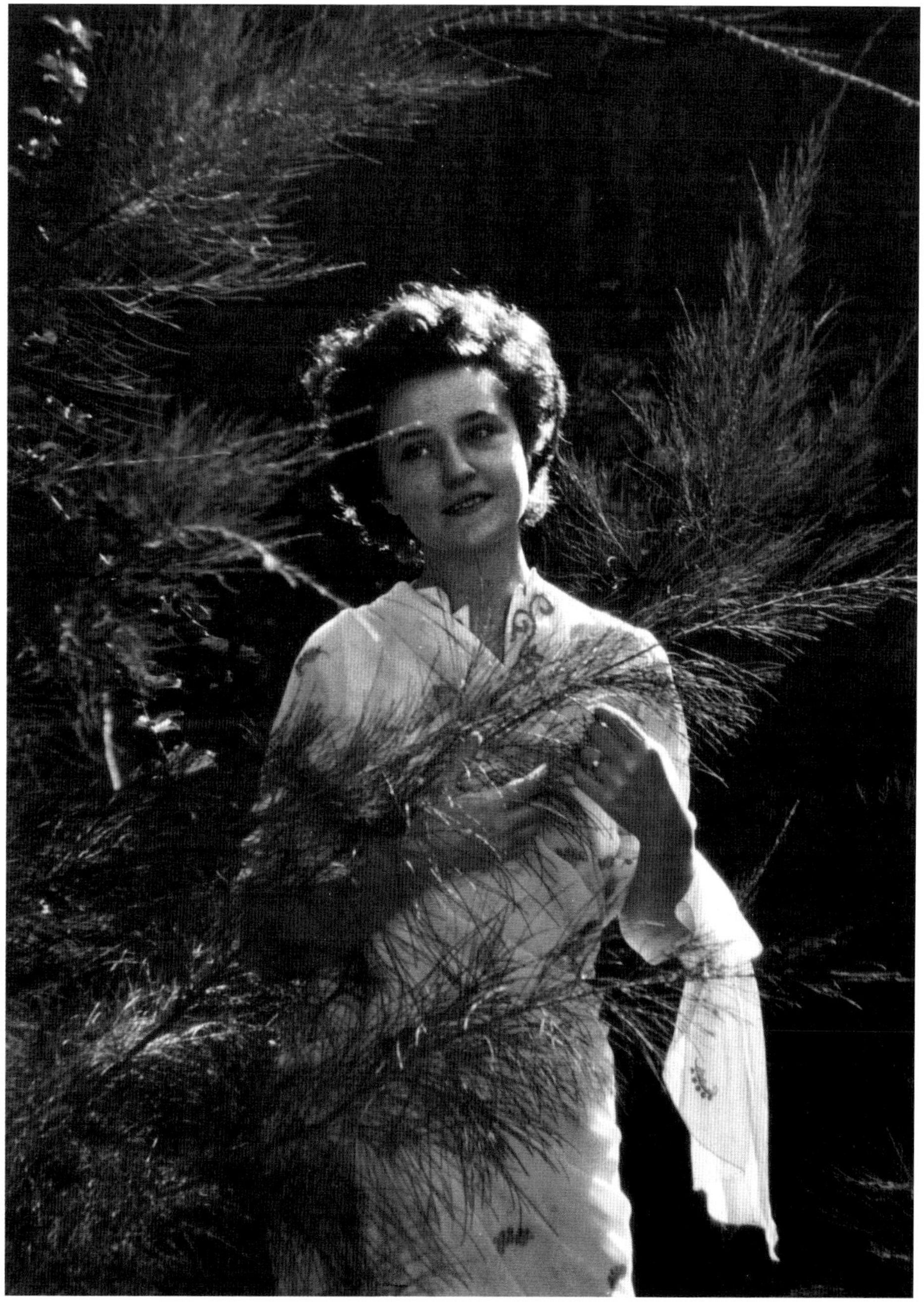

Venkatesh Shirodkar
Sri Aurobindo Ashram, Pondicherry
[Untitled Portrait], c. 1948 - 1975
Gelatin Silver Print, 295 x 218 mm
ACP: D2004.82.0019

BIOGRAPHY OF PHOTOGRAPHERS

Compiled by Jennifer Chowdhry

BOURNE & SHEPHERD

The Bourne & Shepherd studio was initially founded in 1863 in Simla, by Samuel Bourne, a bank clerk and a keen and extremely competent amateur photographer, newly arrived from England, along with William Howard, already an established professional Calcutta-based studio photographer. The studio started trading under the name Howard and Bourne, but by 1864, they were joined in partnership by Charles Shepherd, a well-established photographer. Subsequently, Howard no longer appears in the partnership, and the firm becomes Bourne & Shepherd. Further branches of the studios were established in Calcutta in 1867 and Bombay in 1870. The firm Bourne & Shepherd published a number of catalogues of *Photographic Views in India* along with a catalogue on studies of the racial types. At its peak, it was the most successful commercial firm in 19th and early 20th century India, with outlets in London and Paris, and also ran a mail order service. Bourne left India in 1870, followed by Shepherd who appears to have left the country by about 1878, leaving the firm active. The studio still continues to function in Kolkata under Indian ownership, making it one of the oldest running studios in the world.

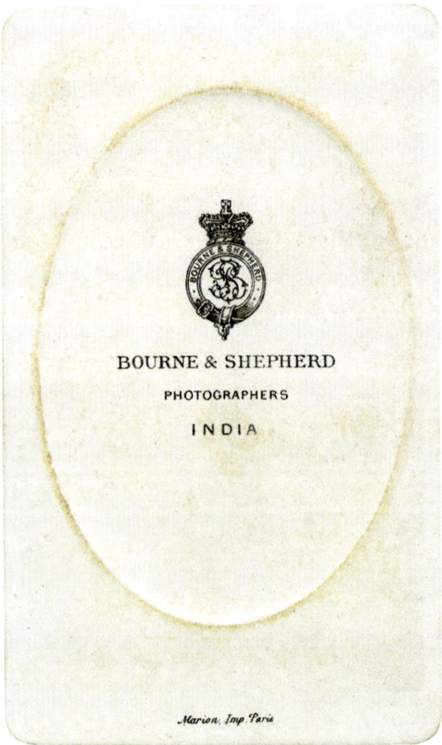

C. (POSSIBLY CHARLES) MOYNE

Moyne was probably a French photographer who worked in South India. The exhibition catalogue *The Colonial Eye: Early Portrait Photography in India* (published by Koehler & Amelang, Leipzig 2012) cites that he ran a studio in Pondicherry in the 1860s. Some images from Calcutta have also been attributed to him in the auction catalogue *The East Indies: Rare Travel Photographs from the Nineteenth Century* (Bernard J. Shapero Rare Books, London).

HENRI CARTIER-BRESSON (1908-2004)

Considered to be the father of photo-journalism, Cartier-Bresson was born in Chanteloup-en-Brie (France) of prosperous middle-class parents. Cartier-Bresson's early training in art (for two years, he studied painting in a Paris studio) helped develop a subtle and sensitive eye for composition. This was seen as one of his greatest assets as a photographer. In 1947, along with Robert Capa, George Rodger and David "Chim" Seymour, Cartier-Bresson formed Magnum Photos. Assignments for major magazines took him across Europe, the United States, India, Russia and China. He visited India in 1947-48, 1950 and again in 1966. His images of the funeral of Mahatma Gandhi won him the Overseas Press Club Award. Many books devoted to his photographs were published in the 50s and 60s; the most famous being *The Decisive Moment* (1952). Cartier-Bresson died in Céreste (Alpes-de-Haute-Provence, France) at the age of 95.

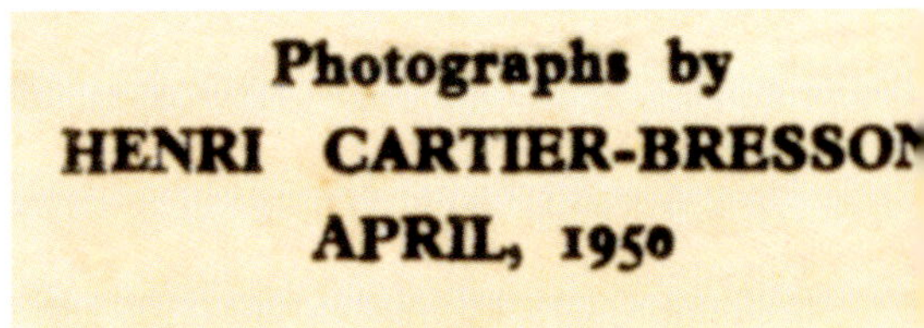

VENKATESH SHIRODKAR (1914-2010)

He joined the Aurobindo Ashram as a young man and gradually took up photography in the Ashram. He was a self-trained photographer, a painter along with being a good cricketer. He then left the Ashram for a few years to get married and later returned to pursue photography. He is survived by his two daughters, Sujata and Pratibha who live in the Ashram.

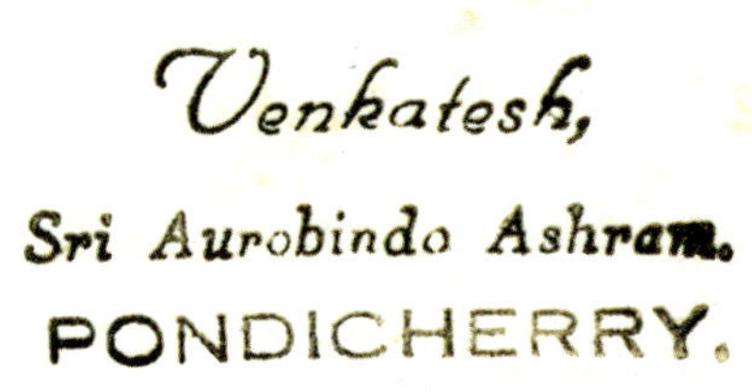

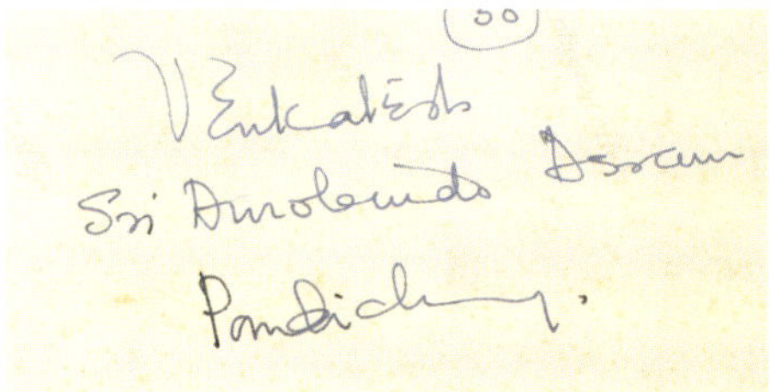

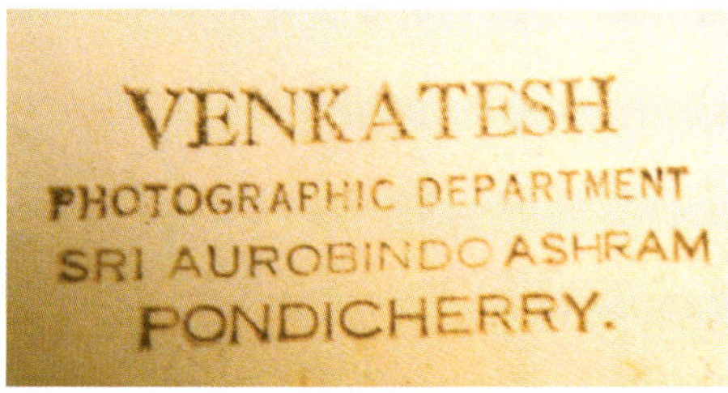

TARA JAUHAR
(B. 1936-)

She joined the Ashram at Pondicherry in 1943 at the age of eight. Tara grew up and received her education at the Ashram's school. Her main interest in photography was to be able to assist in the documentation of the Ashram, its activities and its people. Being very close to the Mother, she photographed a majority of the surviving images of her.

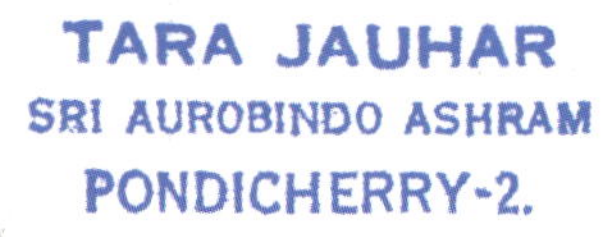

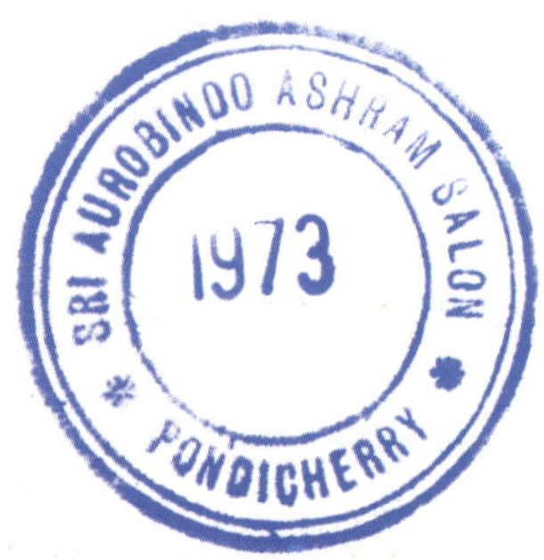

These pictures of the Mother were distributed to the followers. Furthermore, she had a particular fondness for shooting children. She left Pondicherry at the age of 41 and came to Delhi in 1976 to spearhead the work at the Delhi branch of the Ashram, along with her father, Shri Surendra Nath Jauhar. Tara Jauhar is also the author of *Growing Up With the Mother* (Sri Aurobindo Ashram Trust, Pondicherry, 1999) and *The Mother: Selected Photos* (Sri Aurobindo Ashram Delhi Branch Trust, New Delhi, 2009).

PRANAB KUMAR BHATTACHARYA
(1923-2010)

He was born in Behrampore, a district town 116 miles north of Calcutta. From his early childhood, Pranab was interested in sports. Affectionately called Dada, he first came to the Ashram in 1942 and settled there in 1945. A close confidant of the Mother, he learnt all about Sri Aurobindo's yoga and his teachings from her. When the Mother came to know of his interest in photography, she gifted him a camera. Along with Tara Jauhar, he clicked many images of the Mother. He headed the Department of Physical Education and Photography in the Ashram, helping in the selection of images for a bulletin published by the Ashram on physical education.

VIDYAVRATA
(1919-1999)

He joined the Ashram at a young age and took up photography. He did a lot of experiments with his camera and used trick photography to capture some of his images, i.e. by incorporating the technique of superimposition, double exposure and collage. Many of his photographs were published in Indian magazines like the *Illustrated Weekly of India*, *Dharmyug* and *Saptahik Hindustan*, to name a few. He also participated in the Berlin International Photographic Exhibition held in 1960 and was awarded the Pondicherry State Award in 1997. He is survived by a son and a daughter, named Devanshu and Lys, respectively. His son lives in Madras (now Chennai) and has the repository of images shot by him.

FONDATION

H·C·B

Henri Cartier-Bresson

A few years ago Henri Cartier-Bresson, Martine Franck and their daughter Mélanie decided to create the Fondation Henri Cartier-Bresson. Recognised in 2002 by the French Government as being of public interest, the foundation opened its doors in May 2003.

WHY A FOUNDATION?

- To preserve the independence and legacy of Cartier-Bresson's work.
- To retain an exceptional body of work in France.
- To show the public, via exhibitions, the « highlights » of the collection and the work of other photographers, painters, sculptors and illustrators.
- To enable researchers to carry out their studies with more ease.
- To provide support to new photographic projects by organising, every two years, the HCB prize, awarded by an international jury.

THE LOCATION

The Foundation was set up in an elegant artist's studio in Montparnasse, built by French architect Moliné in 1912, winning a prize in 1913 and renovated by the architect's firm Ceria and Coupel. As well as two carefully curated exhibition rooms, the public has access to the third level. This beautiful space with a listed atrium window is a place to relax, while at the same time providing information and audiovisual material amongst a permanent exhibition of a selection of Cartier-Bresson's work.

THE COLLECTION

The collection is made up of original prints, drawings, publications, correspondence, rare books, albums, films, videos, posters, etc. This constitutes the artistic heritage of the Foundation.

As in the past Magnum Photos continues to manage the distribution of Cartier-Bresson's images as also exhibitions which are also part of the foundation's collection.

THE PROGRAMME

Neither museum, nor mausoleum the Foundation is open to other artists. This distinctive feature results in high quality exhibitions of artists whose work follows the vision upheld by Cartier-Bresson. The two exhibition spaces at the Foundation show in turn work by Henri Cartier-Bresson and that of other artists, at the rate of three exhibitions per year. On the third level, films and documentaries on Henri Cartier-Bresson are projected daily. On the fourth level, the archives bring together books, publications, newspaper and magazine article etc. This space is open upon appointment to researchers.

HOW THE FOUNDATION WORKS

The Foundation is privately financed. To help it carry out its projects it must therefore find partners to restore perfectly its collection and curate quality exhibitions with accompanying catalogues.

How you can benefit from the Foundation, in addition to its international reputation: private viewings of the exhibitions, holding of private events on its premises organisation of conferences; financial deductibility : the Fondation Henri Cartier-Bresson is recognised as being of public interest in France and the United States. Consequently all donations originating from those countries are tax deductible.

THE FRIENDS OF THE FONDATION

By becoming a member of the Friends of the Fondation, you will help the Foundation to successfully carry out its projects and you will participate in keeping Henri Cartier-Bresson's legacy alive. Furthermore, joining the Friends of the Fondation will entitle you to visit the Foundation for a year, free of charge. You will also be first informed of upcoming events, enjoy preferential rates on books and catalogues from the bookshop and will be invited to exhibition openings. The benefactors will be offered the publications of the Foundation.

SELECT BIBLIOGRAPHY

Allana, Rahaab and Pramod Kumar K.G. *Painted Photographs: Coloured Portraiture in India*. New Delhi: The Alkazi Collection of Photography and Mapin Publishing, 2008.

Allana, Rahaab (Ed.). *Aperture and Identity: Early Photography in India*. Mumbai: Marg, 2009.

Architectural Heritage of Pondicherry: Tamil and French Precincts. Pondicherry: INTACH Pondicherry Chapter, 2001.

Bate, David. *Photography: The Key Concepts*. Oxford: Berg, 2009.

[By an Officer of the Madras Artillery]. *Notes on Pondicherry; or The French in India*. Calcutta: W.Thacker and Co., 1845.

Curtis, Verna Posever (Ed.). *Photographic Memory: The Album in the Age of Photography*. New York: Aperture, Library of Congress, 2011.

Davenport, Alma. *The History of Photography: An Overview*. Boston: Focal Press, 1991.

Dinkar, Niharika (Ed.). *Framing Women: Gender in the Colonial Archive*. Mumbai: Marg, 2011.

Edwards, Elizabeth. *Raw Histories: Photogprahs, Anthropology and Museums*. Oxford: Berg, 2001.

Edwards, Elizabeth. *Raw Histories: Photographs, Anthropology and Museums*. Oxford: Berg, 2001.

Falconer, John. *India: Pioneering Photographers 1850 – 1900*. London: The British Library and The Howard and Jane Ricketts Collection, 2001.

Falconer, John and Satish Sharma. *A Shifting Focus: Photography in India 1850-1900*. The British Council and British Library Publishing, 1995.

Forrest, G.W. *Cities of India: Past and Present*. Mumbai: English Edition, 1999.

Gadebusche, Raffael Dedo, Katrin Specth and Ludger Derenthal (Ed.). *The Colonial Eye: Early Portrait Photography in India*. Berlin: Staatliche Museen zu Berlin, 2012.

Hight, Eleanor M. and Gary D. Sampson. *Colonialist Photography: Imag(in)ing Race and Place*. London: Routledge, 2002.

Lafont, Jean-Marie. *Chitra Cities and Monuments of Eighteenth-century India from French Archives*, New Delhi: Oxford University Press, 2001.

Llewellyn-Jones, Rosie (Ed.). *Lucknow: City of Ilusions*. London: The Alkazi Collection of Photography and Prestel, 2006.

Mitter, Partha, Akshaya Tankha, Suryanandini Sinha and Rahaab Allana. *The Artful Pose: Early Studio Photography in Mumbai c. 1855 – 1940*. New Delhi: The Alkazi Collection of Photography and Mapin Publishing, 2010.

Michell, George (Ed.). *Vijayanagara: Splendour in Ruins*. New Delhi: The Alkazi Collection of Photography, 2008.

Nilsson, Sten. *European Architecture in India 1750-1850*. London: Faber and Faber, 1968.

Nori, Claude. *French photography: From Its Origins to the Present*. London: Thames and Hudson, 1999.

Pinney, Christopher. *The Coming of Photography in India*. London: The British Library, 2008.

Pinney, Christopher. *Camera Indica: The Social Life of Indian Photographs*. London: Reaktion Books, 1997.

Ramaswamy, Sumathi (Ed.). *Beyond Appearances: Visual Practices and Ideologies in Modern India*. New Delhi: Sage, 2003.

Sharar, Abdul Halim. *Lucknow: The Last Phase of an Oriental Culture*. New Delhi: Oxford University Press, 1975.

Sinha, Arvind. *The Politics of Trade: Anglo-French commerce on the Coromandel Coast 1763 – 1793*. Delhi: Manohar Publishers, 2002.

Weaver, Mike (Ed.). *British Photography in the Nineteenth Century: The Fine Art Tradition*. USA: Cambridge University Press, 1989.

Wells, Liz (Ed.). *The Photography Reader*. Oxon: Routledge, 2003.

Wells, Liz. *Photography: A Critical Introduction*. Oxon: Routledge, 2009.

ACKNOWLEDGEMENTS

On behalf of the Alkazi Foundation for the Arts, I would like to thank all the institutions that have generously shared their resources for the realisation of both, the exhibition as well as this publication. To begin with, discussions on the project began with Mr Jean-Philippe Bottin, Director of the Alliance Française de Delhi, who has kindly hosted the exhibition in the Delhi premises. A very special thanks to H.E. Mr François Richier, the French Ambassador to India and Max Claudet, Counselor for Cooperation and Culture, Embassy of France, India, for supporting the publication and the endeavor as a whole.

This publication would not have reached its current state without support and permissions from the Henri Cartier-Bresson Foundation in Paris, and particularly the assistance of Ms. Aude Raimbault. In a similar vein, we would like to thank the Sri Aurobindo Ashram for permitting us to publish parts of the album by Bresson, as well as providing an enlightening written text on the history of photography there by Prof. Kittu Reddy. The interviews conducted by our archivist Shilpi Goswami with two surviving photographers, Robi Ganguli and Tara Jauhar, has made a distinct intervention on the discourse of Modern Photography in India—we greatly appreciate the time they have taken.

We acknowledge and admire the tireless efforts of Mr Bipin Shah from Mapin Publishing, and his committed team that has managed to pull this publication together in a brief spell of time.

I would also like to extend our gratitude to our colleague in London, Stéphanie Roy-Bharath for her help with the identification of photographs and other texts in the catalogue.

Rahaab Allana

CURATOR, ALKAZI FOUDNATION